ABOLITION AND CAPITAL PUNISHMENT

AMS Studies in Modern Society; Political and Social Issues: No. 16

Other Titles in This Series:

ISSN 0275-8407

ABOLITION
AND
CAPITAL
PUNISHMENT

The United States' Judicial, Political, and Moral Barometer

By

ROGER E. SCHWED

AMS PRESS, INC.
New York, N. Y.

Library of Congress Cataloging in Publication Data

Schwed, Roger E.
  Abolition and Capital Punishment.

  (AMS studies in modern society; no.16)
  Bibliography: p.
  Includes index.
  1. Capital punishment—United States. I. Title.
II. Series.
  KF9227.C2S33   1983   345.73'0773   82-74275
  ISBN 0-404-61623-2   347.305773

MANUFACTURED IN
THE UNITED STATES OF AMERICA

For My Parents

Acknowledgments

The support of my friends has been instrumental in enabling me to commence and finish this manuscript. I would like to thank Tom, Judy, Steve and Stephen in particular, and to extend special gratitude to Susan. As the saying goes, "you know who you are."

I would also like to express my appreciation to Mrs. Otis in Princeton's History Department Office, and to Eric Goldman, for his guidance, instruction, and friendship.

And finally, I would like to acknowledge the loving support of my family: Mom and Dad; Kathy and Eric; Greg; and Laura.

Special thanks and much love go to Mary.

TABLE OF CONTENTS

        Killers should go to
prison in chains and come
out in a box.

                N.J State Senator,
                Joseph Azzolina

                        The treatment of crime
                and criminals is one of the
                most unfailing tests of the
                civilization of any country.
                        Winston Churchill

CHAPTER ONE

> If the beast who sleeps in man could be held
> down by threats--any kind of threat, whether
> of jail or retribution after death--then the
> highest emblem of humanity would be the lion
> tamer in the circus with his whip, not the
> Prophet who sacrificed himself.
>
> Boris Pasternak, Doctor Zhivago

Ever since Cain killed Abel, the human world has been filled with killings and murders and the desire to punish the same. It has not always been the case that the state or government was involved. In primitive early societies, revenge or compensation was usually a matter of self-help, effected by individuals. Relatives or friends of the aggrieved party took it upon themselves to exact payment from the perpetrator, in order to even out matters. To fail to do so meant disgrace and the opprobrium of one's neighbors and society. As a consequence, if the murderer was not available to be punished, his relatives or companions were held liable. These beliefs, embodied by a long tradition, manifested themselves in what were labeled "blood feuds."

The blood feud was simultaneously a stabilizing and a disruptive force for society. On the one hand, it clearly satisfied a well-ingrained and recognized human desire for vengeance, and in this sense, provided a necessary outlet for feelings that stemmed from victimization. Yet on the other hand, it was uncontrollable. Valuable and frequently scarce human resources were squandered in all out fighting that might continue for generations between clans or families. It was inevitable that a governing power, aghast at seeing its tax and army base steadily diminished, would attempt to control the blood feud.

The Development of English Law

By the time of William the Conqueror in England, the state had assumed the power of retaliation on behalf of the injured party. At first, this practice only embraced the concept of revenge, merely substituting the state as judge, jury, and executioner.[1] By instituting a system of fines initially known as the "Danegeld,"[2] though, a further purpose was served, and the homicide rate was substantially reduced. A murderer or his family could escape the revenge dictated by the code of lex talionis[3] and simply pay off wrathful relatives according to the "value" of the deceased. Thus, if a man slew a freeman, he might have to make recompense of a hundred shillings, but if he killed a slave, he would only be

obliged to make a nominal payment to the King, in recognition of disturbing the King's "mund."[4] If a slave killed
his master, though, his life would be forfeit, for he
had no property with which to "satisfy" his victim's
relatives.[5]

As a system of writs and procedures grew out of this
process, the state's intervention had clearly begun to
serve an additional goal, that of deterrence. By regu-
larizing and increasing the certainty of punishment,
the system of state-imposed revenge inevitably implied
protection for society at large by reducing the possibility of committing crimes with impunity. The State, by
assuming the administration of justice, gave everyone a
stake in society as potential aggrieved persons, who
would want a smooth and orderly process to exact their
revenge.

It was not until the time of Henry II (1154-1189),
though, that the notion of a certain punishment being
"deserved" for the commission of a particular crime came
into vogue.[6] Earlier, state-exacted retribution had
merely been the imposition of society's forces on a personal level, to arbitrate between the guilty and the injured parties. The development of the concept that a
criminal offense was not merely a matter between individuals,

but also a crime against the state, was new, and paved
the way for the idea that state punishment for certain
behavior was a moral imperative in itself, and not just a
means of controlling the blood feud. As a result, the
people as a whole became involved in what had formerly
been personal disputes, and the interests of the involved
parties became subordinate to those of society _qua_ avenger.[7]

The potential for tyranny and persecution in this
system was acute. The definition of what constituted
criminal behavior was necessarily left a fluid matter, subject to the whims and preferences of the governing power.
In this manner, heresy and witchcraft, although lacking
specific victims, were punishable actions within a repressive society.

Meanwhile, death as a state imposed punishment was
increasing, being deemed eminently suitable for what
were now the several aims of penal theory: 1. deterrence,
both in a specific and general sense; 2. a suitable punishment befitting the crime; 3. appropriate atonement
to the society and the victim.[8] In particular, as the
importance of the general deterrent function was stressed,
the penalty of death was applied to a widening variety
and scope of crimes, including even the cutting down of
a tree![9] The proportionality and severity of punishment

(including torture) in relation to the crime was considered
secondary if that same punishment was seen as adding to
the intimidation of prospective criminals. Unfortunately
for the ill-liked and poor of England, deterrence theory
was not very far advanced: quite simply, the more severe
a sanction, the more it was thought to deter. By the
time of Henry VIII, no less than two thousand executions
a year were occuring.[10]

The scope of capital crimes continued to expand
straight into the nineteenth century. By 1819 there
were 223 felonies punishable by death in England,[11] and
the list included: "The shooting of a rabbit; the forgery of a birth certificate; the theft of a pocket
handkerchief; the adoption of a disguise;..." and so
on.[12] An undercurrent of leniency in application, however, had by this time ameliorated some of the worst
aspects of the system. Although each year in the early
1800's in England saw between two thousand and three
thousand persons sentenced to death, an execution rate
of only about two to three percent never permitted executions to exceed seventy annually.[13]

The device entitled "benefit of clergy" was a mitigating factor in the sentencing and carrying out of a
death penalty. Originating back in the 1350's in the days

of Edward III,[14] benefit of clergy was an apparatus derived
from the conflict between the state and the church, whereby priests' and other clerics' indictments for felonies
were remanded from secular to ecclesiastical courts.[15]
With time, it was increasingly applied to commoners to
relieve them of death sentences in cases where it was
their first offense, and they proved themselves clergy-
able.[16]

The prerogative of royal mercy, however, was the
main mitigating element. Although the death penalty was
mandatory upon a felony conviction, judges could and did
recommend mercy, and the King in Parliament usually saw
fit to grant it. During the 1790's, more than two-thirds
of all death sentences in England were vacated in this
fashion.[17] A prime motivating force in this pattern of
leniency was the ideas of the Enlightenment, which forced
many to reevaluate penal policy. Perhaps the greatest
change wrought in British thinking in this area was
summed up by the great lawyer Blackstone, who wrote:
"Though the end of punishment is to deter men from of-
fending, it never can follow from thence, that it is
lawful to deter them at any rate, and by any means."[18]
The result was an England which forged ahead of the rest
of Europe in its penal codes and treatment of criminals.

Colonial Transmogrification of British Experience

Colonial criminal statutes were undoubtedly harsh
by modern standards, but surprisingly less severe than
their British heritage might justify. In many ways,
this condition was forged by the uniqueness of the American experiment. Georgia, for example, was founded as
a penal colony for prisoners (debtors in particular)
shipped over from the British Isles. The Pilgrims settled
Massachusetts in hopes of finding the religious freedom
denied them in England. William Penn, under a royal
charter, established Pennsylvania as a Quaker colony. The
novelty of these settlements and some of the new institutions reflected and emphasized the questioning of authority
and power relationships among men that occured in the New
Country. The land was theirs to shape as they saw fit.

It was natural for the colonists in establishing
their criminal statutes to call upon hundreds of years
of British legal experience, and this fact perhaps ex-
plains some of the severity adopted into their penal
codes, for certainly the circumstances of their existence
did not demand it. The lower crime rate and the frequent
shortages of labor would seem to have contradicted the
practicality of executions.[19] Nevertheless, the laws
varied considerably from colony to colony, and in this

sense they reflected each one's perceived needs.

The Massachusetts Puritans, for example, despite their feelings on religious persecution, displayed considerable intolerance in permitting citizens to pursue their own interests free from governmental interference. The Puritans invoked religious Old Testament authority for defining many of their crimes, and by 1647 had evolved a capital code which proscribed practicing witchcraft, cursing one's parents, or just generally being a "rebellious" son.[20]

Virginia, from 1612 to 1619, mandated the death penalty for actions as trivial as stealing grapes or trading with Indians. New York in 1665 defined eleven capital crimes as far ranging from denying the King's rights, to striking one's parent (only if both complained), to premeditated murder.[21]

The more southern colonies, with their interest in preserving order in societies where black slaves outnumbered their masters, maintained harsher codes. As one historian noted: "The death penalty served not only to protect and control the institution of slavery in the South, but also to articulate white supremecy in the social order."[22] In North Carolina, death was required for all of the following crimes: concealing a slave with intent to free him;

the second offense of forgery; circulating seditious literature among slaves; "crimes against nature" (buggery, sodomy, bestiality); arson; and many more.[23] Part of the reason for the maintenance of such harsh codes was the lack of any penitentiaries. Because the few county jails were inadequate and insecure, executions, along with fines and mutilations, were deemed the best way to control the criminal population.[24]

Some colonies did maintain less severe capital statutes. Rhode Island, always an innovator with Roger Williams around, permitted capital punishment for arson and robbery, but not for "blasphemers, idolators, adulterers, and fractious children." Moreover, a particularly enlightened provision excused "fools" and those who "steal for hunger" from the death penalty.[25] Pennsylvania, with its heavily Quaker population, limited capital punishment solely to treason and murder in William Penn's Great Act of 1682.[26] Unfortunately, though, the English Crown defeated these humanitarian efforts in the early 1700's by forcing the adoption of a severer penal code. Typically, by the time of the War of Independence, most colonies mandated death at least for murder, treason, piracy, arson, rape, robbery, burglary, and sodomy. At the same time, the theocratic aspects of most codes were dropped.[27]

After the Revolution

The effect of revolutionary ideology and republican
ideas initially had very little impact on the movement
for reform of the criminal justice system. No doubt the
cruelties of war blunted the finer sensibilities of
persons, so that hangings appeared less gruesome than previously. Many, perhaps reasonably so, saw little or no
contradiction between the goals and rhetoric of the War,
and the administration of American criminal justice.
Certainly the larger discrepancy between the maintenance
of the institution of slavery and the concepts expressed
in the Declaration of Independence deserved (and to some
extent got) more attention.

It took the dissemination of the ideas of the Euro-
pean Enlightenment to instigate agitation for penal reform.
The Italian jurist Cesare Beccaria (1738-1794) and his book,
On Crime and Punishment, received the most attention,
though the works of Montesquieu and Voltaire were influential too.[28] It was Beccaria, for example, who wrote
that "Every act of authority of one man over another,
for which there is not an absolute necessity, is tyrannical."[29]

Perhaps the first American to try to turn these words
into concrete action was Dr. Benjamin Rush, a Philadelphia
physician, who in 1787 called the death penalty an "absurd

and un-Christian practice," and called for its complete
abolition.[30]   His treatise, entitled "The Effects of
Public Punishments upon Criminals and upon Society," was
America's first reasoned argument stressing the impolicy
and injustice of the death penalty for murder, and the
idea that its implementation exceeded governmental powers.[31]
Rush instead encouraged the development of "Houses of
Reform" wherein criminals could be detained until rehabilitated.

Supported by the attorney general of Pennsylvania,
William Bradford, an investigation was undertaken as to the
necessity and utility of capital punishment in Pennsylvania.
Bradford proposed the modern definitions of first and second degree murder and argued that "the source of all human
corruption lies in the impunity of the criminal, not in the
moderation of punishment."[32]   In 1794, Pennsylvania suc-
cumbed to the appeal of Rush's and Bradford's arguments
and retained the death penalty only for first-degree
murders.[33]

Pennsylvania's example spurred on reformers in other
states, particularly New York, where in 1796 the number of
capital crimes was reduced from thirteen to two, treason
and murder being retained (although the degree distinction
was not made).   In the next two decades reform followed

along similar lines in a handful of states. In all of them,
suitable prisons were constructed to house criminals who
formerly would have been executed.[34]

The early 1800's saw new developments, and the first
real pressures for total abolition of the death penalty.
In this respect, the new penal code proposals written under
the auspices of the Louisiana legislature were crucial.
Lawyer Edward Livingston (who would be Secretary of State
under President Andrew Jackson) wrote the commissioned
reports, and intelligently and eloquently called for "the
total abolition of capital punishment."[35] Although his
arguments were lost on the Louisiana public officials,
their publication and wide circulation in 1833 had a profound impact on rising abolitionist movements elsewhere.
So-called "anti-gallows" societies were cropping up everywhere, and more often than not, they borrowed and quoted
extensively from Livingston.[36]

The religious revivalism of the era contributed to
the abolitionist mood, and most debate was on a moral and
theological level. Clergymen in large numbers denounced
in moral terms the "state-sanctioned killings" which constituted capital punishment. The Commandment "Thou shalt
not kill" reverberated from their pulpits. More orthodox
ministers, like George Cheever, appealed to divine

authority, such as Genesis 9:6, to argue just the opposite:
"Whosoever sheddeth a man's blood, so shall his blood be
shed."[37] Notably lacking in this time period was any
stress on utilitarian arguments about the death penalty.

Perhaps it was the special sense of destiny that had
permeated American civilization which gave rise to this
phenomenon. A predominant colonial outlook during the
Revolutionary War had been that America was the last bas-
tion of liberty in the world, fighting against the corrupt-
ness and tyranny of the British King, Parliament and Min-
istry to preserve morality and freedom in government.
Similarly, the rhetoric of the upcoming Civil War would
lend itself to such idealism. Prohibition in the twentieth century would be couched in similar phraseology.
Though it is beyond the scope of this thesis, it is important to stress that the great crusades in American history
for the most part have readily lent themselves to envision-
ing the opposing sides strictly in moral terms, often to
the exclusion of recognizing other motivations. Thus
the abolitionist debates in the early 1800's tended to
underemphasize any considerations of deterrence theory
or effective penal policy.

Which is not to say they were unsuccessful. Rather
the atmosphere of the 1830's and 1840's thrived on such

argumentation. Abolitionist Robert Rantoul, Jr. struck
on an archetypal chord of human thought in pronouncing
"a man holds his life as a tenant at will, --not indeed
of society, who did not and cannot give it, renew it,
and have therefore no right to take it away, --but of that
Almighty Being whose gift life is..."[38] Absolutism began
to take on a full head of steam.

In 1837, Maine became the first state, in effect, to
declare a moratorium on the death penalty. The Maine
law, partially in reaction to the riots and unruliness that
had accompanied a recent public hanging, provided that a
warrant for execution could not be issued until at least
one year after the sentencing date of the criminal, and
then, only by the Governor. This allocation of responsibility squarely onto the executive's shoulders had the
desired result: no executions.[39]

The territory of Michigan in 1847 was the first
state to really abolish capital punishment. With no executions since 1830, the area's politicians simply brought
Michigan's laws into conformity with practice. Although
capital punishment was retained for "treason against the
state," that was a rather unusual crime, to say the least.[40]
The example of Michigan, combined with the abolitionist
urgings of Horace Greeley's influential New York Tribune,

spurred on reform efforts elsewhere. In 1852, Rhode Island
eliminated the death penalty except for persons convicted
of murder while serving a life sentence.[41] Wisconsin
followed with total abolition the very next year, but
more due to a gruesomely bungled public hanging and an
anti-capital punishment jury acquittal of a clearly guilty
party.[42] Elsewhere, states sought to reduce the number
of capital crimes, and by the time of the Civil War, three-
fourths of them had made robbery and burglary non-capital.[43]

The moral and political energies of the abolitionists,
however, were soon absorbed into the Civil War as many,
like William Lloyd Garrison, recognized slavery to be the
greatest evil plaguing the land. The post-war abolitionist activity was sporadic. The severe cruelties of the
war rendered insignificant for many the executions of persons who were, after all, convicted murderers. Nevertheless, Maine abolished (1876), restored (1883) and re-abolished (1887) capital punishment during this period. Iowa
toyed with abolition for six years from 1872-1878. Colorado
abolished for an even shorter span, from 1897-1901. Kansas
experienced de facto abolition in 1872, and then wrote it
into law in 1907. Meanwhile, the Federal government in
1897 was reducing the number of federal capital offenses
from sixty to three (murder, treason, and rape), and was

providing juries with sentencing discretion in murder and
rape cases.[44]

Abolition in the Twentieth Century

Abolitionist furor experienced a complete revival
in the conducive atmosphere of the Populist and Progressive
Eras. No less than seven states -- Minnesota (1911),
Washington (1913), Oregon (1914), North and South
Dakota (1915), Tennessee (1915), Arizona (1916), and
Missouri (1917) -- abolished the death penalty for murder.[45]
By 1917, twelve states were in the abolitionist corner,
and six others had gotten a ban through at least one
house of their legislatures. Reform organizations such
as the Anti-Capital Punishment League headed by Charles
Ingersoll and the Anti-Capital Punishment Society of
America headed by Arizona Governor George Hunt, were turn-
ing up everywhere, and the issue was before the public
more than ever before.[46]

The form of discussion was evolving, too. Though
Genesis 9:6 was still being tossed back and forth, the
deterrence issue was coming to the fore. Retentionists,
without any particular proof, were stressing the intuitive
logic of the proposition that fear of death would deter
the most people from crime. Abolitionists, employing

an increasingly scientific view of criminals and prisons, were arguing the opposite.[47]

The onset of World War I was a major setback for abolitionists and has to be considered the main contributing factor towards the restoration of capital punishment in five states and the failure of reform in many others. Historian Phillip E. Mackey analyzed the trend thusly: "The reform climate could hardly have been worse than in the period 1918-1920. War psychology and anticipation of a crime wave combined with hatred of immigrants and fear of radicalism to produce a virtual hysteria among the American people."[48] Fear of the Industrial Workers of the World (IWW), for example, appeared to be the prime causal factor for the narrow victory of an Oregon public referendum restoring capital punishment in 1920. Always, one or two particularly violent crimes would serve to reverse public and legislative opinion. Such seems to have been the case in Washington when in 1917 a murderer of a leading businessman openly "boasted that he would be sent to the pen for life to be fed and cared for" at public expense.[49] Additionally, the lesson supposedly learned in Colorado never seemed to be far from legislators' minds. There, retentionists argued, abolition had been the direct

cause of several lynchings afterwards.[50] The public
would not stand for mere life imprisonment of murderers
it was contended, and though no one explicitly said so,
the fact that these criminals were predominantly black,
foreign and poor did not hurt either.

It was lean times for abolitionists, as their pleas
fell upon deaf ears. The New York Times was beginning
to reconsider its support of the death penalty, but not
in a very positive fashion: "While the abolition of
capital punishment might not be wise, it would be less
unwise than leaving the matter as it is, with death
the penalty for murder only in instances when juries think
it has been earned by what they consider special atrocity."[51]
Clarence Darrow, perhaps the most persuasive abolitionist
spokesman of the period, achieved no small feat in 1924
in saving Nathan Leopold and Richard Loeb from execution,
and getting them life sentences. These two young and
wealthy Chicagoans had committed a particularly atrocious torture murder 'for kicks,' and while the abolitionists claimed a victory, the public-at-large was angered
to see these two child-murderers escape death.[52]

Somewhat encouraged nevertheless, a mixed bag of
prominent abolitionists, including Darrow, went on to
form the American League to Abolish Capital Punishment.

A national body, the League supported abolition legislation all over the country. The Sacco and Vanzetti
execution in 1927 greatly swelled its membership ranks, and
the League went on to keep the issue of capital punishment
alive and viable in a basically unreceptive climate.[53]
Yet the depression years, followed by World War II, the
McCarthy Era and the Korean War, barely gave the abolitionists breathing space. Although the number of executions gradually declined from a high in 1935 of 199 to
only 56 in 1960,[54] no new legislative bans on executions
were won. Delaware abolished in 1958, but rapidly restored in 1961 despite the Governor's veto and a lower
murder rate during the three year moratorium. Two particularly heinous crimes involving young blacks killing
elderly whites seem to have provided the impetus.[55]
At a time of heavy racial tension, with all eyes on the
desegregation at Little Rock and the civil rights protest
elsewhere, the reintroduction of the death penalty in
Delaware has to be construed as a form of racial legislation aimed at the Negroes who were committing a disproportionate percentage of homicides in relation to the
percentage of the total population they comprised.[56]

By 1960, though executions in America were on the
decline, the abolitionists really had not made much

headway in challenging the actual legitimacy of capital
punishment as law. Whereas in 1917 fully one quarter
of the states outlawed the death penalty, by 1960 (Delaware excluded), only eight states still saw fit to ban
executions.[57] Nevertheless, the steady downward trend
of executions indicated that all was not lost. While
Americans obviously did not wish to relinquish capital
punishment as an alternative, the decreasing number of
death sentences carried out was evidence of a greater un-
willingness to follow through with an actual execution.

In general terms, this reluctance to execute appears
attributable to several causes. Statistician William
Bowers' regressional analysis shows that for most of
the country, except the South, the execution rate declined
most precipitously during the 1940's.[58] This evidence
suggests that perhaps the Nazi atrocities of World War II
made Americans think twice about their use of capital
punishment, especially in reference to the United States'
claims of moral superiority. The Northern states with
sizable groups of persons with German extraction may have
been rendered particularly sensitive to this point.[59]

The South, however, which was accounting for more
executions than the rest of the country put together,
did not really start slowing its pace of execution until

the early 1950's. The perseverance of capital punishment in the South after the 1940's can be explained to the
extent that the death penalty is seen as racially aimed
legislation (particularly in cases of blacks raping whites).
The diminishment of capital punishment in the 1950's,
however, was probably based on the growing receptivity
of higher courts to appeals in capital cases, whereby
prisoners and their lawyers were being encouraged to file
writs of habeas corpus.[60] A growing pile of empirical
evidence, moreover, was for the first time demonstrating
the discriminatory nature of the death penalty as applied
in the South. Concerned lawyers and the NAACP's Legal
Defense Fund began to represent as counsel an increasing
number of death row prisoners. Taken together, the
greater amount of appeals and legal representation, along
with the growing evidence of discrimination, discouraged
officials from carrying out death sentences too rapidly.[61]

For the nation as a whole, it was clear that the
people with the actual burden of processing an execution
(judges, governors, and prison authorities) were the ones
jamming up the country's death rows. For most people, the
death penalty had actually been made more palatable,des-
pite abolitionist agitation, due to reforms slowly but
consistently being initiated throughout the history of

capital punishment.

Reforms in Capital Punishment

Execution methods perennially were being refined
to minimize complaints of painful and/or gruesome killings.
The early colonial experience had included burning at the
stake and pressing to death.[62] Hanging, the prevailing
mode of execution up through most of the nineteenth
century, had its flaws too. It took considerable skill,
which many hangmen did not have, to correlate the weight
of the body to the length of the drop so that on the one
hand, the person died quickly, but on the other, his
head remained attached to his corpse. Even carried out
properly, hung people were known to struggle for upwards
of ten minutes.[63]

The introduction of the electric chair in New York
State in 1889 was hailed as a step towards truly "humane"
killing by the state. Willie Kemmler was the first to
die in "the chair" (1890), but even his execution did not
procede smoothly. Current was applied for seventeen
seconds and then turned off, but still being alive, he
was given an extra four seconds of electricity.[64] Future
cases of electrocution were often so prolonged that the
corpse actually would "roast" and emit foul odors of

burning flesh.

Nevada was the next state to succumb to the search for innovative techniques of execution, and in 1921 passed a bill to execute condemned prisoners with a lethal dose of cyanide gas. In 1924, Gee Jon was the first person to "benefit" from this discovery, and a Nevada newspaper editorial hailed the event: "It brings us one step further from the savage state where we seek vengeance and retaliatory pain infliction."[65] Abolitionists, of course, would contend otherwise. The search for so-called "civilized" execution techniques can really be seen as merely a conscience-assuaging process, which in lessening the pain suffered by the criminal, minimizes the public outcry against capital punishment. Even today, the search continues. Oklahoma in 1977 passed legislation providing for a lethal injection to be given Death Row inmates, Texas and Idaho followed suit in 1978, and similar bills are pending in four other states.[66]

The same sort of rationalization has characterized the elimination in America of the public execution. Theoretically if capital punishment is touted as a deterrent, public executions would seem logically to maximize this effect. They never worked as intended though. The story goes that when pickpocketing was a capital crime in England, the pickpockets plied their trade on the crowd that came to watch a hanging for the very same offense.[67] But particularly objectionable to authorities was the mob scene that inevitably occured at each public hanging. Drunken revelry, fighting and obscene conduct were all commonplace, and seemed to lend credence to the theory that executions had a brutalizing effect on society.[68] Consequently, executions were turned into private affairs before a few witnesses. By the 1830's they were a rarity, although the last public execution in America was not until 1936, in Kentucky, before a crowd of 20,000 persons.[69] The net result of this reform is perhaps best expressed by the old adage "out of sight, out of mind." Abolitionists certainly could not complain about the "humanity" of removing death from the public eye, but the reality was that Americans became increasingly out of touch with the cold cruel realities of the execution process, and were able to condone capital punishment more easily.[70]

Another reform which served to build a buffer between the citizens of the United States and the criminals they were voting to kill was the movement of executions from under the aegis of local authorities to that of the state. This trend began in 1864 with Vermont and Maine,

and reached a peak from 1890 to 1920, when some 32 jurisdictions completed the change.[71] Ostensibly the cost of the
electrocution apparatus necessitated this transition, but
the net effect was the infusion of an even greater element
of impersonalization into the death process.

The reforms that damaged the abolitionists' goal of
total repudiation of the death penalty the most, however,
were the two which seemed to the public to make the application of capital punishment more just: the definition
of degrees of murder; and discretionary sentencing. The
splitting up of the crime of murder into different cate-
gories (i.e. first-degree, second-degree, manslaughter,
etc.) as noted previously, was initiated by Pennsylvania
in 1794. Most other states followed within the next few
decades. Such a distinction permitted legal officials
and the public to accept capital punishment with even less
qualms because now it was argued that only those really
"deserving" of death (pre-meditated and felony murders)
would be executed. Even abolitionists preferred to see
this reform rather than none at all, but the public confidence it inspired in the judicial system made their job
all that much harder.[72]

The transformation of most mandatory death penalty
statutes into ones permitting jury-sentencing discretion

also served to alleviate some of the severity and inequity in the application of capital punishment, and again,
made the abolitionists' ultimate goal all the more difficult to attain. The historical inadequacy of mandatory statutes was legendary. Legislatures, in prescribing the attributes of what constituted an action "punishable by death," necessarily took into their net of
capital crimes more criminals than was either just or
desirable. The inevitable result was "jury nullification"
or "pious perjury," where in defiance of their oaths,
jurors would acquit a guilty party whom they did not
want seen put to death.[73] This practice was prevalent
in antebellum America and widely deplored. As one Rhode
Island newspaper complained, "Unless the prisoner, from
his color or extraction, is cut off from ordinary sympathy, he is almost sure of an acquittal."[74]

Benjamin Porter, a member of the Alabama House
of Representatives in 1884, attempted an explanation:
"This is because men have more humanity than the society
which they establish. Because as a society, they must
enact laws, which in the next moment they abrogate, in
consequence of their inconsistency with the unconquerable
feelings of our nature."[75] Tennessee, in 1838, was the
first to correct this "inconsistency" by ceding to the

jury full sentencing discretion in capital offense cases.
Alabama followed in 1841, Louisiana in 1846, and eighteen
other states in the years 1860 to 1895.[76] The idea was
to get more convictions, even at the sake of fewer death
sentences, and it worked. Abolitionists were once again
stuck with a reform of the criminal justice system which
they could hardly argue against, but which would undoubtedly eliminate many reservations people had against applying the death penalty.

By 1960, the death penalty was firmly entrenched
in American society. Despite the declining number of
executions, capital punishment's legitimacy per se as law
was going virtually unchallenged. The small but persis-
tent group of abolitionists had proven unable to reverse
this trend. Fully fifty-one percent of the population
favored capital punishment, as compared to thirty-six
percent who were opposed.[77] Death sentences were being
handed out in greater numbers, and the legislatures,
impervious to abolitionist lobbying and petitioning attempts,
were not even reviewing or reappraising their policies.
In the whole United States, with more than 7,000 legal
executions since 1900, only ten states (three with any
depth of seriousness) had sponsored investigations into

the policy considerations of the death penalty. The
Federal Government had been totally quiet in this area.[78]
Great Britain, by comparison, in 1866, 1929-1930, and
1949-1953, had supervised three different and massive
enquiries into the desirability of capital punishment.[79]

In essence, the issue of capital punishment in
America was surrounded by what abolitionist Hugo Adam
Bedau termed a "conspiracy of neglect and silence." The
responsibility for maintaining the death penalty was
widely diffused among the public, legislators, prosecutors,
jurors, trial judges, appeal courts, and governors, and as
a consequence, no one group felt a pressing need for
change. Juries could pronounce death sentences secure
in the rationalization that theirs was not the last word.
As Legal Defense Fund (LDF) lawyer Anthony Amsterdam said,
"the result of this process is that at the end somebody's
dead, and nobody killed him."[80] There was no reason to
suspect that the next decade would be any different -- but
then, America had never experienced anything exactly like
the Sixties.

CHAPTER TWO

> I shall ask for the abolition of the pun-
> isment of death until I have the infallibility
> of human judgment demonstrated to me.
>
> Thomas Jefferson

A prerequisite to a fuller comprehension of the recent history of the death penalty and the reasons for its various observable trends, is a knowledge of the arguments which form the basis of the capital punishment controversy. In particular, the focus of the debate in the past two decades has subtly altered in reaction to new needs. The injection of the death penalty dispute into the court system has placed a heavier emphasis on the utilitarian aspects of the dispute, and has spurred the creation of a growing body of empirical evidence. Previously the stress in discussion had been on humanitarian and moral considerations, but the recognition that such beliefs were less subject to change and could not be the sole basis for judicial adjudication, forced a revised approach.

The abolitionist contention that all human life is sacred quite simply is not going to convert people who don't believe it, nor is it going to convince a court or legislature that such a tenet is the appropriate foundation for decision-making. Similarly, retentionist arguments derived from Genesis 9:6 or lex talionis will be persuasive only with people who are inclined to see matters in that fashion. To the extent that such immalleable moral convictions are at the core of attitudes towards capital punishment, rational discussion of pros and cons serves little purpose. Yet conceivably, either moral position could be embodied in the laws of the land, the dilemma is merely to choose which one. If one starts from the legal position that the life of a criminal can be taken if it saves the lives of innocents, a dialectic on the utility of capital punishment as policy then becomes all important. It is this direction that the dialogue on capital punishment must take.

Deterrence

> The inhibiting effect of sanctions on
> the criminal activity of people other
> than the sanctioned offender.[1]

The question of the deterrent efficacy of capital punishment is central to any reasoned discussion on the merits of the death penalty. Advocates of capital punishment generally maintain that the death penalty deters more murderers than life imprisonment does; abolitionists generally argue that the effects of the two sanctions are equal. The obvious questions under these circumstances are: "Who is Right?" and "How can an answer be determined?"

One approach has been to rely on empirical evidence generated by statistical analysis. The pioneer in this type of study was Thorsten Sellin. Sellin's 1959 report used the homicide rates in abolition states from 1920-1963 and compared them to those in contiguous death penalty states. He attempted to control for other factors affecting homicide rates by matching states with similar social, economic and cultural characteristics. His interpretation of his data was: "The inevitable conclusion is that executions have no discernible effect on homicide death rates..."[2]

Sellin also did a time series analysis on the effect of abolition and reintroduction of the death penalty on homicide rates within any one state.[3] His results were similar: "If any conclusion can be drawn, it is that there is no evidence that abolition of the death penalty generally causes an increase in criminal homicides or that its re-introduction is followed by a decline. The explanation of changes in homicide rates must be sought elsewhere."[4]

One other frequently cited study by Sellin involves

the question of whether or not policemen are safer in
states that have kept the death penalty, as some retentionists claim. Again, using similar analytic techniques,
Sellin found no statistically significant differences
among states. Approximately 1.3 policemen per 100,000
population were killed in retentionist states, and 1.2
policemen per 100,000 population in abolitionist states.[5]

Other studies have tended to reinforce Sellin's findings. Robert Dann, proceeding on the theory that a deterrent effect would show up following an execution, chose
five years (1927, 1929, 1930, 1931, 1932) in which Philadelphia had an execution both preceded and followed by
60 days completely free from executions. Collapsing the
five periods together, Dann found that there were 91
homicides before the executions, and 113 afterwards, the
opposite of what one would expect.[6]

A modification of Dann's approach was undertaken
by Leonard D. Savitz. Savitz hypothesized that perhaps the
deterrent effect is more related to publicity, in which
case the pronouncing of a death sentence during a trial
would be more important as a deterrent than the actual
execution itself. Duplicating Dann's procedures except
for this distinction, Savitz concluded however, that
"...There emerges ... no pattern that would indicate

deterrence."[7]

At face value, these five studies are useful, but
they are by no means conclusive. As a group, they all
suffer from important methodological flaws. Because the
available crime rates the reports rely on do not distinguish between capital and noncapital homicides, there is
no way of being certain that a deterrent effect on capital
homicides is not simply being covered up by an increase
in the noncapital homicides. More importantly though,
despite Sellin's effort to match states with similar characteristics, there are simply too many demographic, cultural, and socioeconomic factors which affect homicide
rates to be able to conclude anything definitely. In Dann's
study, for example, perhaps the rise in homicides would
have been even more marked if the death penalty had not
been used.

More recently, economist Isaac Ehrlich, who claims to
have avoided the above pitfalls by using econometric analysis that controls for other factors, studied the period
from 1933-1969 and concluded: "An additional execution
per year... may have resulted on the average in seven or
eight fewer murders."[8] This rather impressive trade-off
statistic, however, cannot be said definitely to exist.
Like the studies showing no deterrent effect for capital

punishment, Ehrlich's report suffers severe shortcomings.
Of particular consequence is the high sensitivity of his
results to the time period chosen. If one lops off the
last five years included in his study, his deterrent effect simply disappears. Moreover, Ehrlich completely
fails to account for the rise in homicide rates in recent
years in the context of rising crime rates in general.
Additionally, his rather unique regression analysis is
somewhat suspect; if one substitutes a normal linear regression analysis, all of Ehrlich's results again vanish.[9]

What is evident about statistical studies on deterrence is that they resolve very little. As the National
Research Council's Panel on Research on Deterrent and
Incapacitative Effects concluded in 1978: "The panel
considers that research on the deterrent effects of capital sanctions is not likely to provide results that will
or should have much influence on policy makers."[10] Or as
Professor Charles L. Black Jr. observed: "A 'scientific'
-- that is to say, a soundly based -- conclusion [on
deterrence] is simply impossible, and no methodological
path out of this tangle suggests itself."[11]

In the face of this lack of proof one way or another,
both sides have tried to claim an advantage. Some retentionists have fallen back upon Judge Hyman Barshay's

intuitively appealing but logically specious "lighthouse"
example:

> The death penalty is a warning, just like a
> lighthouse throwing its beams out to sea. We
> hear about shipwrecks, but we do not hear about
> the ships the lighthouse guides safely on their
> way. We do not have proof of the number of
> ships it saves, but we do not tear the light-
> house down.[12]

Of course, the analogy entirely begs the question. Abolitionists do not deny that the death penalty serves as
a deterrent, but rather they ask for evidence that the
death penalty is a _superior_ deterrent than life imprisonment.[13] We might tear down the lighthouse if it had
tremendous costs _and_ we knew a man holding a flashlight
could do the same job.

Slightly less transparent as logic is criminologist
Ernest van den Haag's contention that in the absence of
convincing evidence either way on deterrence, society
must face two risks: 1. if the death penalty doesn't
deter, we execute condemned convicts and forfeit their
lives; 2. if the death penalty does deter, and we fail to
execute anyone, we lose the lives of innocents killed by
would-be-deterred murderers. Given this choice, van den Haag
argues, he would prefer to take the first risk.[14]

Van den Haag's syllogistic approach is appealing at

first, but falls to the same abolitionist argument. The
burden of proof is on the retentionists to show the marginal (added) deterrent effect of capital punishment over
life imprisonment, particularly with a punishment that
has been used only twice in over fifteen years against
anyone who didn't desire it, and which is wholly different
from any other sanction society employs.

Imagine if the punishment being considered was torture followed by death. Van den Haag's two risks would be
essentially the same: 1. if torture and death do not deter, we inflict great pain upon our condemned convicts,
and forfeit their lives; 2. if torture and death do deter,
and we fail to employ them, we lose the lives of innocents
killed by would-be-deterred murderers. Yet in this case,
van den Haag would clearly be required to prove that the
extra increment of severity in punishment has a corres-
ponding increase in deterrent effect. So it should be in
justifying the death penalty over life imprisonment.
Society is not justified in mandating a quantifiably different and harsher penalty (and few would dispute that
death in comparison to a prison term fits this description) unless its benefits are positively and affirmatively
demonstrated.

Retentionists have sometimes attempted to meet this

burden by arguing from personal experience and relating anecdotes where criminals have modified their illegal actions in order to avoid the death penalty. Into this category fall tales of robbers who tell the police that they used simulated or unloaded guns out of fear of the death penalty. Is this, then, the necessary proof that the death penalty deters?

The answer is no for several reasons.[15] First, an arrested person will generally tell the police what he thinks they want to hear. After conviction, interviews of the same men by experienced officials like Warden Duffy of San Quentin reveal that the death penalty did not deter them at all. One such convict admitted that "well, I said that because it seemed like a good thing to say at the moment."[16]

Second, a robber might not carry a working weapon for a very good reason: he does not wish to kill. Not all robbers are murderers, and many would consider taking a life in pusuance of money to be morally unjustifiable.

Third, even if one accepts these arrested persons' statements at face value, all they show is that a heavier penalty deters more. In abolitionist states, for example, robbery suspects without working weapons will simply say that they did not wish to risk life imprisonment.

Even if there are specific instances where the death
penalty has seemed to be a better deterrent, they are more
than offset by the number of well-documented cases where
the existence of the death penalty has actually been an
incentive to "suicide-types" who commit murder.[17] The
American Psychiatric Association, for example, announced
that there was evidence that the death penalty "... creates
a breeding gound for psychosis in death row -- exhibition-
ists, suiciders [sic], to whom the lure of danger has a
strong appeal."[18] Gary Gilmore was the most recent and
famous example of this type. Gilmore's psychosis and dis-
torted sense of machismo was evident in many of his actions.
Besides attempting suicide twice while in prison, he requested: a death row wedding; the firing squad instead
of the hangman; to be spared the blindfold; and a six-
pack of Coors beer as his last meal.[19] Dr. John C. Woods,
chief of forensic psychiatry at Utah State hospital, tried
to describe Gilmore's problems:

> I think that shortly after Gary got out
> of prison he knew within himself that he was
> not able to make it in society. Knowing he
> did not want to return to prison, he took the
> steps necessary to turn the job of his own de-
> struction over to someone else.
> He went out of his way to get the death
> penalty; that's why he pulled two execution-
> style murders he was bound to get caught for.
> I think it's a legitimate question, based on

this evidence and our own knowledge of the
individual, to ask if Gilmore would have killed
if there was not a death penalty in Utah.[20]

The personality that commits "suicide through murder"
surely does exist, and strongly suggests that the death
penalty in cases actually works as a counter-deterrent
to encourage crime! The point being that even _if_ capital
punishment _had_ a marginal deterrent effect over life imprisonment, that advantage would be more than offset by
the homicides spurred on by the death penalty.[21]

Perhaps the greatest reason for the persistence of
the deterrence theory notion, however, is its appeal to
common-sense psychology. If men fear death above all else,
then certainly the threat of death must deter. Retentionists commonly argue along these lines. Edward J. Allen,
a former chief of police in California, says as much:
"Why does every criminal sentenced to death seek commutation to life imprisonment? Common sense alone... convinces that we are influenced to the greatest degree by
that which we love, respect or fear to the greatest degree..."[22]
The variations on this theme are numerous: "Human nature
being what it is, potential criminals are most effectively
deterred from crime by what they fear the most."[23] And so
on.

The intuitive appeal of these propositions is great,

but fails to stand up to more careful thinking. First of all, it is the _imminence_ of death that really frightens, and not the abstract concept. Otherwise, everyone would go through life terrified, knowing they were eventually going to die. And as statistics show, the imposition of the death penalty is no sure thing, even after one has committed murder. When executions in this country were at a peak in the 1930's, no more than approximately one out of seventy homicides was punished by death, and this figure translates to only about one out of ten capital crimes. In the Fifties, the risk for murderers was still less: about one out of one hundred and one out of sixteen, for homicides and capital crimes respectively.[24]

Furthermore, if a criminal considers risk, his chief danger of death from crime is not execution, but being killed by a policeman or citizen during the crime's commission. A Chicago study showed that between 1934 and 1954, policemen killed 69 and civilians killed 261 homicide suspects. During these same years, Chicago witnessed forty-three executions.[25] Thus, a state with the death penalty doesn't greatly increase the risk of death for a criminal.

It is unrealistic, moreover, to represent murderers as generally weighing and balancing these sorts of considerations. Generally, homicide is a crime in _fers brevis_, or "the heat of passion," within families or between acquaintances, where neither a decision to kill, nor an evaluation of the possible consequences, is consciously reached.[26]

The picture of people who might be deterred from murdering because of capital sanctions, then, has shrunk considerably. What one is left with is those who weigh the risk of punishment in the case of getting caught, and consider the risk of death too great for the anticipated gain of the crime, while that of lengthy incarceration is not. The authors of The Ceylon Report on Capital Punishment observed:

> It would be most exceptional for a man to be insufficiently sane and normal to be deterred by the risk of a sentence of protracted imprisonment but yet sufficiently sane and normal to be deterred by the risk of his own execution, when both risks are at a level of contingency which he is doing his utmost to avoid."[27]

As Justice Brennan wrote in his Furman opinion, "the assumption that such persons exist is implausible."[28] What is particularly upsetting for abolitionists is that given these rather overwhelming arguments against the deterrent effect of capital punishment, fully 93% of death penalty proponents nevertheless believe in it.[29] The implication is that either the public is uninformed, or just not convinced.

Retribution

Retribution as an argument in favor of capital punishment simply means one thing: criminals should be put
to death because they deserve it. The appeal of this
proposition is undeniable. As Arthur Koestler, author of
Reflections on Hanging has observed: "The desire for vengeance has deep unconscious roots and is roused when we
feel strong indignation or revulsion -- whether the reasoning mind approves or not."[30] As such, retributive in-
stincts have to be considered perhaps the strongest motivation people have for supporting the death penalty. Fully
two-thirds of capital punishment proponents admit that they
would not change their views even if it was proven to their
satisfaction that the death penalty was not a deterrent.
Almost half would remain adamant even if it were shown to
be a counter-deterrent.[31] A January 1977 CBS Poll indicated
that 66% of the country wanted Gary Gilmore executed, and
that from among those who did not believe his death would
have a deterrent effect, fully 54% still thought he should
die.[32] Conceivably other factors (e.g. fear of recidivism)
could account for these percentages, but no doubt the
retributive impulse contributes a great deal to the public's

support for capital punishment.

From the viewpoint of personal philosophy, whether wishing for vengeance is desirable or not is ultimately a clash of values which cannot be resolved by argument.[33] One simply cannot prove that anyone is "wrong" or "right" in this conflict. What one can prove, however, is that to the extent that revenge is an emotional unthinking reaction, the desire for its imposition should not be the primary guiding force in creating law. As Koestler has argued, such impulses should not be

> ...legally sanctioned by society, any more than we sanction some other unpalatable instincts of our biological inheritance. Deep inside every civilized being there lurks a tiny Stone Age man, dangling a club to rob and rape, and screaming an eye for an eye. But we would rather not have that little fur-clad individual dictate the law of the land.[34]

The concept of the law as it has developed in the United States is antithetical to the idea that emotional caprice can be the sole foundation of legislation. Laws pertaining to punishment can and do recognize the existence of retributive desires, but they are supposed to restrict and constructively channel such impulses, rather than timidly to sanction and encourage them.

This conclusion is inescapable in the light of modern day penological goals. In 1949, Justice Black wrote for

the majority of the Supreme Court that "retribution is
no longer the dominant objective of criminal law. Re-
formation and rehabilitation of offenders have become
important goals of criminal jurisprudence."[35] Revenge
undeniably _is_ a factor in choosing to punish criminals,
but it must be taken in conjunction with the other aims
of penology: 1. general deterrence; 2. incapacitation of
the offender; 3. rehabilitation of the offender.

As Justice Marshall wrote for a divided court in the
1972 case of _Furman_ v. _Georgia_: "The fact that the State
may seek retribution against those who have broken its
laws does not mean that retribution may then become the
State's sole end in punishing."[36] Yet capital punishment,
in that it eliminates the possibility of rehabilitation,
but does not improve over life imprisonment in the areas
of deterrence and incapacitation, then becomes punishment _simply_ for punishment's sake. This idea is in ac-
cord with neither modern penology nor law.

Some retentionists nevertheless will argue that
purely retributive justice does have a role. Mayor Ed
Koch of New York, for example, said "I believe...that society has the right to demonstrate its sense of moral
outrage at particularly heinous crimes."[37] The fallacy
of this approach, of course, is that other sanctions, like

life imprisonment without parole, are equally capable of
satisfying "moral outrage."[38] The appropriate retributive punishment to express "moral outrage" really reduces
to being a matter of opinion, and suggests inabilities of
purely retributive law to deal evenly with each case. If
one advocates the notion that society should execute those
who deserve it, the question of "Who deserves it?" is raised. If one then contends that the "seriousness" or "atrocity" of a crime will determine "who deserves it?"
subjectivity and arbitrariness will still remain in the
determination of what constitutes an heinous crime.[39]

There is still the further question as to whether
capital punishment as actually practiced in the United
States can be a satisfactory fulfillment of the retributive impulse. First, to the extent that the desire
to kill someone for revenge diminishes with the time
elapsed after his offense, the long delay between the ap-
prehension of a suspect and his execution may entirely
subvert the goal of retribution.

Second, to the extent that vengeance demands that
the deceased's friends or relatives carry out the retaliatory action themselves, state-imposed executions again
may fail to satisfy the retributive impulse. No way out
of these two dilemmas seems apparent without sacrificing

notions of due process.

Finally, the fact that "the overwhelming number of criminals who commit capital crimes go to prison..."[40] suggests that the desire for revenge might be undermined when only a few scapegoats are executed. As Charles Bryant, a rapist on Death Row in Louisiana says, "Look at guys like Charles Manson -- mass murderers -- who'll be eligible for parole in seven years or so. Is it fair that they get life and me death?"[41] A small and highly random sample of people who are executed while others convicted of identical crimes are simply imprisoned indicates the problems of capital punishment as a method of retributive justice.

Arbitrariness and Discrimination

As the above suggests, one of the main arguments against capital punishment in America is the nature of its imposition. Abolitionists contend that the whole process, from arrest to execution, divides those who are going to die from those who are going to live on the basis of decisions made "...under no standards at all or under pseudo-standards without discoverable meaning."[42] Furthermore, there seems to be no acceptable method within the foreseeable future of limiting this unchecked discretion.

An analysis of the process a suspect typically
undergoes in getting from the street to the "chair" will
highlight the inability of the United States criminal
justice system to administer rationally and even-handedly
the penalty of death.[43] First, the prosecutor has to
charge the crime. He is not guided in this choice by
any particular standards, and may decide to prosecute a
homicide as a capital charge because of any number of
variables, including political pressures. Next, the decision whether or not to plea-bargain has to be made.
Factors he may weigh here are: the trial resources at
that particular time (plea-bargaining is a necessity due
to overcrowding of the court system); the likelihood of
winning the case (most prosecutors like to maintain a
"good winning percentage"); the defendant's "respectability"
or standing in society; and again, political pressures.
Of course, the importance of the defendent having a good
lawyer at this stage of the proceedings cannot really be
overemphasized. The net result, then, is that some continue along the path to execution here, while others exit,
and not by any "repeatable" application of standards.[44]
Nor does it seem clear that the process by which these
decisions are reached can ever be reduced to regularized
rules of law.

The next stage is the findings of the jury, and here
again, decisionmaking is infused with an uncontrollable
amount of individual discretion that inevitably imposes
arbitrary results. First, the jury can find the defendant guilty on a lesser, non-capital charge. But to do
so, they have to interpret psychological evidence, physical facts, and mitigating circumstances. What was the defendant's mens rea or mental state? Was the crime pre-
meditated? Is the claim of temporary insanity exculpa-
tory? In particular, this last finding lends itself to
inconsistent results. The celebrated "McNaghten rules,"
established in an 1843 English trial, shed little clarifying light. The secretary to the Prime Minister was
mistaken for the Prime Minister and assassinated by
McNaghten, under the delusion that the Prime Minister was
responsible for McNaghten's personal and financial mis-
fortune. The rules provide for a ruling of insanity if
the offense was the result of a "...defect of reason
from disease of the mind," or one did not "know the nature
and quality of the act he was doing," or "if he did know
it... he did not know that he was doing wrong."[45] It is
hard to argue that these sorts of instructions provide
anything beyond a framework for disguising jury discretion.

Jury sentencing procedures, too, suffer from the same

lack of definable standards. The consideration of the
aggravating and mitigating circumstances of an offense
permits each jury to exercise its own opinion as to what
constitutes a reason for granting mercy or not. Even the
new and supposedly more restrictive death penalty
statutes, generated by the Supreme Court's Furman decision, are required only to "...focus the jury's attention
on the particularized nature of the crime and the particularized characteristics of the individual defendent."[46]
The Texas death penalty statute (held constitutional --
see Jurek v. Texas (1976)), for example, provides only
that the jury determine "...whether there is a probability
that the defendant would commit criminal acts of violence
that would constitute a continuing threat to society" (emphasis added).[47] Needless to say, the definitions of
"probability" and what constitutes a "continuing threat to
society" are not axiomatic. Is probability a 51% chance
or a 90% chance? Do future robberies constitute a "continuing threat" or do only future murders? Can any of
these matters be decided "beyond a reasonable doubt," as
the law requires?[48] These sorts of provisions are completely
unworkable if the law is concerned with dispensing even-
handed results. Mandatory statutes, as the history of
capital punishment shows, are not the solution either (nor

are they any longer considered constitutional -- see
Woodson v. North Carolina (1976)). The inescapable conclusion, then, is that the meting out of death in America,
short of the total abolition of capital punishment, will
continue in a haphazard and capricious fashion.

The clemency process is the ultimate re-affirmation
of this conclusion. Governors and pardon boards are required to follow no set pattern in commuting death sentences. They have the power over life and death, and it
is controlled only by an individualized sense of duty
which can set a priority either on what the public wants,
what the courts have held, what a conscience dictates, or
all, none, or any of these considerations. Governor Dunn
of Tennessee, as a lameduck in 1972, commuted all the
death sentences in the state to life.[49] On the other
hand, Governor Richard Hughes of New Jersey, despite personal qualms about the death sentence, signed two death
warrants during his tenure.[50] Thus, in addition to the
fact that different states, for similar crimes, have different statutory penalties, the commutation power of governors means that death relies on a sort of geographical
lottery, where the "wrongness" of one's crime is a reflection of the state it occurs in.

In operation, all the above characteristics of the

law combine to produce a system of justice "...in which
a few people are selected, without adequately shown or
structured reason for their being selected, to die."[51]
Since 1930 there have been over 400,000 reported criminal
homicides (of which approximately 15% are capital), but
only 3334 executions for murder.[52] As the Washington Research Project report concluded: "As the system of capital punishment now operates, the law could as well provide
that persons committing capital crimes shall be sentenced
to play Russian Roulette with a fifty or hundred chambered
revolver."[53] Even people who believe in the retributive
and deterrent aspects of capital punishment might wish to
alter their positions in light of this evidence.

Retentionists reply, however, that even if arbitrariness is the rule, that in itself is no indictment of
capital punishment per se, but merely a condemnation of
the system which imposes death. As an argument, they
contend, caprice and arbitrariness apply equally to all
punishments. Change and reform court and criminal procedure,
retentionists conclude, but do not throw away capital punishment merely because it, like other punishments, is
sometimes imposed unfairly.

Abolitionists of course, see matters from a different
viewpoint. They contend quite simply that death is different

from all other punishments. As Professor Charles L. Black,
Jr. of Yale argues: "We ought not to accept, with respect
to the death penalty, the arbitrariness and fallibility
in decision which we must accept, and will no doubt go on
accepting, with regard to other punishment."[54] In a legal sense, due process requirements necessarily increase
where death is an issue. As the late Justice Harlan wrote
in an opinion, "so far as capital cases are concerned, I
think they stand on quite a different footing than other
offenses.... I do not concede that whatever process is 'due'
an offender faced with a fine or a prison sentence necessarily satisfies the requirements of the Constitution in
a capital case."[55] To cease using the system to impose
executions, then, does not mean a commitment to abandon
criminal punishment all together. Simply, as Black con-
cludes, "In law, as in life, death is supremely different."[56]

A corollary of the above arguments is the contention
that the death penalty exacts its vengeance unduly from
among the ranks of the poor. If a defendent is rich, he
can post bail, stir up and motivate people to dig for favorable evidence, and most importantly, hire a good lawyer.
The options for the poor are simply not comparable. They
have to sit in jail and depend upon court-appointed counsel
(often overworked and unpaid) to create and plead their

case.

From the plea-bargaining, to the trial, to the appeal,
there can be little doubt that it clearly matters as to
whether one has a great lawyer or a mediocre one. With inevitable results, the poor get the mediocre lawyers. As
former Governor DiSalle of Ohio observed: "The men who
occupied death row... during my administration had one thing
in common: they were penniless."[57] The late Warden Lewis
E. Lawes of Sing Sing Prison echoed this sentiment: "In
the twelve years of my wardenship I have escorted 150 men
and one woman to the death chamber and the electric chair
... In one respect they were all alike. All were poor,
and most were friendless."[58] The wealthy, even though
they undoubtedly commit fewer capital crimes, simply are
not represented on death row. As Justice Douglas argued
in his Furman opinion, "one searches our chronicles in
vain for the execution of any member of the affluent
strata of this society. The Leopolds and Loebs are given
prison terms, not sentenced to death."[59] Statistics tend
to confirm these observations. A Pennsylvania study indicated that over 30% of condemned men with retained counsel
received commutations, while less than 20% with court-appointed counsel did. In Ohio, the comparable percentages
were forty-four and thirty-one percent, respectively.[60]

It bears repeating that although the poor are at a disadvantage in any criminal proceeding, in matters of life and death, this bias in the administration of justice becomes unacceptable.

It has also long been contended by abolitionists that the administration of capital punishment in the United States is characterized by racial discrimination. In particular, the percentage of black rape offenses resulting in death sentences, and the percentage of black death sentences resulting in executions, are both disproportionately high relative to the same percentages for white offenders. Additionally, the percentage of blacks who receive commutations of their death sentences is disproportionately low relative to that of white offenders.[61]

The problem of actually _proving_ racial discrimination, however, is somewhat similar to the problem encountered in studying deterrence effects: one has to control for extraneous factors. Thus if one cites the statistic that since 1930, 405 blacks and 48 whites have been executed for rape [62] it would be jumping the gun to contend that these figures prove racial discrimination. First, the disproportionate execution of blacks for rape may reflect the differential offense rates between blacks and whites. Second, it may reflect other relevant legal considerations

associated with the offenses, such as committing the rape
during a burglary. Nevertheless, given the substantial
leeway for discretion which characterizes criminal procedings, and given America's three hundred year history
of discriminatory treatment towards blacks, statistics such
as the one above, even uncontrolled, are highly suggestive
of racial discrimination. For example, since 1930, the
Northeast and the West have not executed anyone for rape.
Eleven southern states, however, have accounted for all
but fifty-six of the executions for rape.[63] Given the
South's less than always hospitable accomodation of blacks,
rape law as repressive class legislation seems a distinct
possibility.

One study in particular has confirmed this suspicion
beyond refutation. The report spans a twenty year period
from 1945-1965, and examines in detail the relationship
between race and sentencing for rape in eleven southern
states where rape was a capital offense. The collection
of the data included non-racial variables potentially affecting sentencing patterns such as: a contemporaneous
offense; carrying a weapon; age and previous record of
the offender; amount of injury to the victim; and so on.[64]
The results were enlightening. In all, two dozen possibly
aggravating nonracial variables were considered, and not

one was of any statistical significance. Only the vari-
able of race could be said to have produced the imposition
of the death penalty in disproportionate numbers upon
blacks.[65] As one researcher summarized: "Over at least
a twenty year period there has been a systematic, differential practice of imposing the death penalty on blacks for
rape and, most particularly, when the defendants are black
and their victims are white.[66] (See tables -- next page.)
The fact that a black rape of a white woman was treated
most severely can hardly come as a surprise considering
the caste values and attitudes of whites in the South,
but this study was the first well-founded statistical con-
firmation.

Evidence exists of racial discrimination in the imposition of death sentences for murder and in the execution of those who receive death sentences, but it is the
result of less thoroughly controlled analyses.[67] However,
the fact that racial discrimination was a major consideration in the execution rate for rapists would logically
suggest that the execution rate for murder cannot be entirely prejudice-free.[68] Blacks, for example, account for
49% of the executions for murder (68% in the South), but
constitute only about 10% of the general population.[69]
Admittedly the black homicide rate is higher than its

Florida Rape Convictions: 1940-1964 [70]

	Defendant		Victim	
	Black	White	Black	White
Number Convicted:	152		68	84
		132	7	125
Electrocutions:	29		0	29
		1	0	1*
Awaiting Execution:	12		2*	10
		0	0	0

*children under 14

Rape: Race of Defendant by Type of Sentence [71]
(for Fla., Ga., La., S. Carolina, Tenn.: 1945-1965)

	Death	Other
Black:	110 (13%)	713 (87%)
White:	9 (2%)	433 (98%)

Rape: Racial Combinations of
Defendant and Victim by Type of Sentence [72]
(for Ark., Fla., Ga., La., S. Carolina, Tenn.: 1945-1965)

	Death	Other
Black defendant, White victim:	113 (36%)	204 (64%)
All other Combinations:	19 (2%)	902 (98%)

white counterpart, but a presumption of racial discrimination is eminently reasonable in light of the rape
study.

More recently, evidence from new research has sur-
faced, and preliminary findings indicate that the race of
the victim is controlling in determining who is sentenced
to death for murder. The study, conducted by Dr. William
J. Bowers, looked at three states (Georgia, Florida, and
Texas) whose total Death Row populations by December 1977
accounted for 225 of the 408 persons on Death Rows throughout the United States. The results showed that while 45%
of the condemned prisoners were blacks who killed whites,
only 5% were blacks who killed blacks. 50% were whites
who killed whites, and none were whites who killed blacks.[73]
As Bowers pointed out, "a majority of murderers have killed
blacks, but only five percent of those on Death Row have
done so."[74] The implications as to the value a predominantly white society places on the lives of its innocent
black populace are self-evident. As for capital punishment,
the evidence for racial discrimination in its imposition
argues for the curtailment of the death penalty's use at
least until more exhaustive studies are conducted. The
suspicions of present findings seem more likely than not
to be confirmed by future research.[75]

Restraint, Reform and Recidivism

Retentionists often argue that the death penalty is the only sure method for protecting society from further crimes by convicted murderers. Capital punishment is the ultimate "specific deterrent" they contend, and ensures that no one murderer will be able to kill again. Of particular concern to death penalty advocates is the granting of a "license to kill" to prisoners already with life sentences who cannot be punished additionally for further crimes. Society would be taking unacceptable risks to permit these condemned inmates to remain alive, or ever to become eligible for parole.

The available evidence suggests that these concerns are unfounded. Paroled murderers present a lower risk to society than any other group of offenders. Numerous studies have examined this risk, and the results have always been the same: "The rate of parole violation for the homicide group is the lowest of any offense category."[76] For example, in New York between 1930 and 1961, sixty-three first degree murderers were paroled, and by the end of 1962, only one had committed another crime (burglary). During the same period, the violation rate for all parolees was 41%, of which 18% were criminal arrests.[77] In California between 1945 and 1954, only one out of 342 first degree

murder parolees was convicted of murder a second time.[78]
In Michigan, of 164 first-degree murderers who were paroled
between 1930 and 1959, only four violated parole, and
only one committed another felony (not homicide).[79]

The inevitable conclusion is that murderers as a
class of criminal offenders are exceptionally well behaved. Michael DiSalle, during his tenure as Governor
of Ohio, completely staffed his Executive Mansion with
convicted killers.[80] It should be remembered that people
who kill are generally not ruthless professionals, but
rather people driven by exceptional situations of stress.[81]
What is too often forgotten is that other convicts, from
traffic offenders to armed robbers, are more likely to
continue lives of crime after parole, and inevitably will
commit some murders too. Yet no one could reasonably argue
that they sould be executed as a preventative to recidivism.

The same can be said of convicts serving life terms.
They rarely do kill in prison, and on the whole, are better behaved than other classes of criminal offenders.[82]
Nor can inmates serving life terms be considered as having
nothing to lose. The possibilities of solitary confinement, later parole, and loss of privileges (cigarettes,
TV, exercise, etc.) have to be considered as negative

incentives to bad behavior for persons whose existence
is confined to a tiny cell. If anything, it should logically be the prisoners on Death Row who would be most uncontrollable and the greatest threat to guards and other
inmates. Realistically, the eruption of prisoner violence
has very little to do with whatever deterrents exist, be
they death or solitary confinement. Rather, repressive
and inhumane conditions, or ill treatment by correctional
officials, spur the release of violence among prisoners.[83]
The Attica uprising in New York, for example, occured despite the state's death penalty provision for the killing
of a prison guard.

In summary, there seems to be no additional protection given to society when murderers are executed rather
than imprisoned. Where parole is unwarranted, incarceration can continue indefinitely. To argue that Parole Boards
cannot be trusted with this function is really no different
than contending that juries will sometimes acquit a true
murderer. Both are the risks of criminal procedings.

More importantly though, execution denies men the
possibility of rehabilitation. The case books are full of
the success stories of the Leopolds, Crumps, and Smiths
who were once considered "unreformable."[84] That a fear of
recidivism (as seen, less justifiable in the case of

murder than in other offenses) should deny the chance of
rehabilitation to hundreds of potentially redeemable men,
bodes poorly for the notion of a "civilized" society.

Irrevocability and the Criminal System

> The whole history of the death penalty in the
> criminal justice system shows it creates a
> great deal of confusion.[85]

> LDF Lawyer David Kendall

Capital punishment creates a debilitating tension
in the nation's legal system. There is an overriding
fear, and justly so, of killing an innocent person, or
one denied due process. As bad as the imprisonment of the
wrong man must be considered, nothing wholly transcends
the horror of executing someone innocent.[86] Yet, as
long as eyewitnesses can make faulty identifications, or
appellate courts can miss violations of a defendant's
rights, the possibility of improperly sending someone to
his death remains.

The irrevocable nature of the death penalty generates
a fear of error, which in turn, weakens the law. As Justice Jackson freely admitted: "When the penalty is death,
we... are tempted to strain the evidence and even, in close
cases, the law in order to give a doubtfully condemned man

another chance."[87] No one wishes to assume full responsibility for someone else's death, and legal loopholes are
opened where there were none before. Judges and juries,
not wishing to impose the death penalty, return verdicts
not directly justifiable by facts or the law.

Capital cases account for a disproportionate amount
of post-trial litigation and consequently strain the resources of the courts. Lawyers will try any and all sorts
of appeals to save their client, and concerned judges will
inevitably pay close attention to them. The issuance of
stays of execution becomes a matter of course as petitioners
argue that new laws or evidence are relevant to their cases.
The list of landmark Supreme Court cases which have freed
hundreds of prisoners for new trials, but could not free
others because they had already been executed, is very long.
Consequently long delays are tolerated so that the risk of
killing a convict who might be affected by other adjudication is diminished. The greatest deterrent aspects of
punishment, swiftness and certainty, are lost.[88]

Yet as long as capital punishment exists, its imposition can proceed in no other manner. The care presently
expended is a tribute to the courts' concern for justice
and due process, but it is also an indicator of the disproportionate costs capital punishment imposes on the
criminal system.[89] A huge allocation of human resources

goes into the administration of a punishment which, at
best, has dubious benefits. Worse, the injection of life
and death issues into the criminal system serves to de-
emphasize the necessity of improving the real backbone
of criminal punishment: imprisonment and rehabilitation
of offenders. When capital punishment is seen as a cure-
all for rising crime, these crucial issues will be substantially ignored.

Brutalization of Society

Retentionists frequently argue that capital punishment is needed to demonstrate the value society places
on the lives of its law-abiding citizens. Thus van den Haa,
contends that "when murder no longer forfeits the murderer'
life, ...respect for life itself is diminished, as the
price for taking it is."[90] In other words, the value of
a human life must be expressed in the willingness of society to take one if necessary.

Similar sentiments are sometimes phrased differently:
"who are you for, the criminal or the victim?" asks one
capital punishment advocate.[91] As J. Edgar Hoover expresse
himself: "We must never allow misguided compassion to eras
our concern for the hundreds of unfortunate innocent victims of bestial criminals."[92] As some retentionists see

the issue, then, if society spares the life of a murderer,
it has effectively forgotten about the victim. The fact
that a murderer may be completely reformable and that taking
his life can do nothing to restore or comfort the victim is
considered unimportant in light of the priority of assert-
ing the value of life through the execution of those who
take it.

It is hard to refute this position as a matter of
logic, but Professor Amsterdam has done a good job of presenting the opposing abolitionist viewpoint:

> Capital punishment teaches the moral that hu-
> man life ceases to be sacred when it is thought
> useful to take it....If we keep a penalty on the
> books which says in effect, that those who be-
> lieve there are pragmatic ends to be served by
> killing other people should be allowed to kill
> them...then we are simply legitimizing violence
> by anyone who thinks it will do some good.
>   What our time needs, however, is just the
> opposite....Violence is largely the product of
> putting too little value on the worth of life.
> The antidote for violence is to emphasize the
> worth of life. To abolish capital punishment
> is to emphasize the worth of life.[93]

The taking of any human life, even that of the worst
mass murderer, is seen by most abolitionists as debasing
to society and the sanctity of life in general. Fundamentally this aspect of the conflict between advocates
and opponents of the death penalty reduces to an irre-
concilable clash of values.

The brutalizing effect of capital punishment on most
everyone the process touches, however, is more readily
confirmable. The very fact that public executions have
been eliminated in the United States is evidence of the
obscene and dehumanizing features of the death penalty.
That the trend has been towards more private and more
humane executions means that whatever effect there is, must
be considered debasing and harmful. Public executions
never seemed to serve very well the purpose of scaring or
deterring would-be wrong-doers. Rather, the event was a
spectacle which attracted thousands, and catered to and
encouraged all the sadistic and subhuman impulses of man.
This brutalizing effect, which permitted mobs to thoroughly
enjoy themselves as recently as forty-seven years ago, should
be considered none the less real simply because of the
privacy of present-day proceedings. The tragedy remains
great for witnesses, those in authority, reporters and
others, and must have an eroding effect on their respect
for basic human values.[94]

The condemned go through tremendous physical and psycho
logical suffering on their way to the execution chamber (see
appendix A). Repeated last minute stays force Death Row
inmates to face the ultimate horror of imminent death time
and time again.[95] The actual execution can mangle and

disfigure their bodies, and inevitably fails to kill them
except after several minutes. The ghastly true stories
which exist are too many to relate here,[96] but are clearly
incompatable with notions holding the dignity of man sacred.
As Camus wrote, "The man who enjoys his coffee while reading that justice has been done would spit it out at the
least detail."[97] Convicted killers are too often treated
not as people, but as things, without inalienable human
rights.

The arguments in this chapter have not meant to be
unbiased, but they have strived to be persuasive in their
reliance on the facts. It is a common belief among abolitionists that if people were only more informed about
capital punishment, the public outcry against its imposition would swell. Yet the evidence supporting this contention of rational thought being determining has not always been conclusive. The Sixties saw many swings in
people's attitudes towards the death penalty, and it is
not obvious that the considerations of this chapter were
always primary causal factors. Nevertheless, the pro and
con arguments in the capital punishment controversy provide an important starting point for analyzing strictly
what happened.

CHAPTER THREE

I want to destroy this myth that those
monsters on Death Row spring full blown from
Hell.

Caryl Chessman

"Mitchell's crime was equalled by two thousand men in our prison population in California.
But they're in the yard.
"Sure that made me feel guilty; but I ra-
tionalized it. I spread my guilt among the ten
million voters of the state. Everybody who could
vote had his hand on that lever. My participation
and guilt equaled one ten-millionth of California.
"I was Buddhistic about the thing. Life is
fleeting at best. We were killing thousands in
Vietnam.

Assistant Warden Jim Park of San Quentin,
after executing Aaron Mitchell.

The Thursday morning headlines of May 3, 1960 let the

whole world know for sure. Caryl Chessman was dead, exe-

cuted in the state of California a few minutes after

10:00 a.m. the day before. There had been no last-minute

stay this time, although eight previous delays had held

out the tenuous thread of perhaps one more, even after

the cyanide pellet had dropped. After twelve long years

on Death Row, the longest such confinement in the United

States' history, Chessman's protracted struggle with the

law was finally over. America's struggle with its con-

science was just beginning.

In retrospect, it is no doubt symbolic that the decade

which was to see some of the greatest upheavals and social
changes in American life was "baptized" after barely four
months by no doubt the most controversial execution since
that of the Rosenbergs. Yet in 1953, the issue was not
so much the appropriateness of capital punishment as it
was the innocence or not of the two accused spies. A
1953 Gallup poll showed that the death penalty for murder
was supported by fully 68% of the public, with 25% opposed.
For treason, these percentages were even more lopsided.[1]
With Chessman in 1960, although his innocence at various
times was contended, the larger controversy of state-imposed death loomed above all else. The pressures to take
or voice a stand on capital punishment were greater.

After what had been a long period of relative dormancy,
abolitionism would take giant strides ahead in the 1960's.
The steps forward were unprecedented in their scope, direction, and number. For the first time since George Gallup
started to earn a living, the country would go on record
as opposing capital punishment. The May 1966 poll revealed that 42% of the United States answered "yes" when
asked "Are you in favor of the death penalty for people
convicted of murder?" but an even larger 47% responded in
the negative. This transformation had been slow, but
steady.[2]

	1953	1960	1965	1966
Yes	68	51	45	42
No	25	36	43	47
No Opinion	7	13	12	11

While abolition forces must have derived tremendous satisfaction from these statistics, the greater thrill no doubt came with the de facto halt of executions in America after 1967, when Aaron Mitchell became the last man in the United States, for a period of over twenty years, to be executed against his will.[3] Here, too, the trend was no less methodical:

Year	1960	1961	1962	1963	1964	1965	1966	1967
Number of Executions	56	42	47	21	15	7	1	2

Thus, in exactly thirty-two years, the United States had gone from 199 executions a year to none.[4]

Anti-capital punishment lobbies also enjoyed their greatest successes in state legislatures since before World War I. Three states completely eliminated the use of capital punishment. Oregon, where a 1958 popular refer- endum abolishing capital punishment had lost by 10,000 votes, did an about-face in 1964, when the measure passed

by more than 150,000 votes.[5] Iowa and West Virginia
simply abolished capital punishment in their assemblies
during 1965. Three other states, New York(1965), New
Mexico(1969), and Vermont(1965), restricted the application of capital punishment to the murder of law enforcement officers in the line of duty (Vermont and New Mexico
also kept a provision providing death for repeat murderers)[6].

Public officials, in positions of power and influence,
gave abolition tremendous boosts by coming out during the
Sixties in favor of ending the death penalty. Hubert
Humphrey, in response to a campaign question in April 1960,
said: "My own personal views are that society should not
be interested in vengeance, but rather in deterrents to
crime. Until it can be statistically proven that the
threat of the death penalty deters crime, I am inclined
to feel that society is better off without it."[7] Ramsey
Clark, as attorney general during the waning months of
the Johnson administration, put the full force of his department behind the abolition of the federal death penalty
statutes, thus reversing his stand of 1965.[8] Perhaps most
surprising was the involvement of the United States Supreme
Court. The Court denied _certiorari_ in the 1963 case of
Rudolph v. _Alabama_[9], but Justice Goldberg along with two

other justices filed a basically serendipitous dissent
for the abolitionists on three unraised issues: 1. does
the death penalty for rape violate standards of decency?;
2. is the death penalty for a crime which does not take a life,
excessive?; 3. if punishment for rape can be achieved with
less, is the death penalty unnecessary cruelty? Many interpreted the dissent as hinting that capital punishment
should be an issue for the courts to consider.

All of the above-described events influenced one
another, and in time, were affected by still other changes
of the Sixties. Court action, for example, was crucial
to halting the executions, while supportive public opinion
generally eased the way for the abolition of the death
penalty in the aforementioned states. Nor can the social
climate of the day be ignored. The Vietnam War, the civil
rights agitation and a general politicization of the populace all have to be considered as significant causal
factors one way or another. Yet if a history is to be
constructed out of this mass of changes, the analysis has
to commence with Caryl Chessman. In essence, Chessman's
ordeal politicized the question of capital punishment.
Whereas previous history demonstrated that the public
and politicians would gladly avoid the matter, the events
surrounding Chessman's incarceration and subsequent death

thrust the issue of capital punishment directly out into
the open for public scrutiny.

"Kill Me if You Can"

The facts of the Chessman case bespeak of a horrible
miscarriage of the law. As one leading criminologist has
said, "to describe Chessman's trial in 1948 as one of the
most fantastic travesties of justice in the history of civilized criminal jurisprudence would involve considerable
restraint in the choice of language."[10] From the beginning,
all the cards in the deck were stacked against Chessman. Los
Angeles was being plagued by a series of crimes committed by
the "Red Light Bandit," so-named because he shone a police
type red spotlight on parked cars in lovers' lanes to
induce couples to unroll the windows or open the doors.
He would then rob them at gunpoint, and in two cases,
forced the women involved to have "sex acts" with him. The
pressure on the Los Angeles police to apprehend this "monster" who was sometimes seen driving a grey car, was immense.
Caryl Chessman, on parole from San Quentin at the time, was
caught while driving a recently stolen grey car one night.
Despite the fact that the "grey car" had been sought for
weeks, that one witness placed Chessman miles away at the
time of the crimes, that the attacked women gave police

conflicting descriptions, and that he had no history of
sexual depravity and was married, Chessman was charged
with being the Red Light Bandit.[11]

Eighteen different felony counts were filed against
Chessman, but the ones that subjected him to the death
penalty under California's "Little Lindbergh Law" were
the two that charged him with "kidnapping for the purpose
of robbery." But is that what actually happened? In the
first case, the Bandit robbed a couple and then ordered
the woman, one Regina Johnson, to move into his car, where
she was forced to perform fellatio. The other crime took
place similarly, except that the bandit first drove several
miles with the victim, Mary Alice Meza, parked, and then
commanded sexual acts, none of which involved any penetra-
tion. These events, then, constituted the "kidnapping" for
purposes of robbery on which Chessman was tried, convicted,
and sentenced to death. And yet it was clear that the movement of the victims was solely for sexual purposes, a crime
admittedly punishable with life imprisonment, but not death.
California's Little Lindbergh Law, a complete garble of
legal language, had been completely misapplied, a point
missed or ignored by the courts in every appeal Chessman
was to file.[12]

The actual pre-trial and trial proceedings were no

less appalling in their lack of adherence to established notions of justice. Mary Meza's identification of Chessman, for example, occured not from a line-up or mug shots, but when a handcuffed Chessman was brought to her house by police. A "confession" introduced at the trial had been obtained only after police had held Chessman incommunicado for three days without a lawyer and had beaten him with a pistol-butt, egregiously illegal practices according to previous Supreme Court rulings.[13]

During the trial, Judge Charles W. Fricke, a notorious "hanging judge," displayed clear hostility to Chessman partially because he was acting as his own counsel. For example, he allowed eleven women to be seated on the jury (which, remember, was to decide on sex charges!). Chessman was always confined to his chair, his objections were perpetually overruled, and he was denied access to the daily transcripts for scrutiny. In his summation, Judge Fricke told the jurors that Chessman's victims had suffered "a fate worse than death" and that if they did not return a death sentence even a life sentence without possibility of parole could be "no positive assurance that [Chessman] would not be free again." The jury's only question to the judge during deliberations was addressed to this point.[14] Of course, to sentence

someone to death solely on an unproven "future protection
of society" basis, besides being purely speculative, rejects
all considerations of rehabilitation. Unfortunately, the
California Supreme Court did not rule this practice unconstitutional until 1964, four years too late for Chessman.[15]

The greatest injustice inflicted on Chessman, though,
concerned his trial transcript, an accurate copy of which
would be essential if he were to have any success in proving
to the appellate courts the unfairness and prejudice which
permeated his conviction. Mr. Perry, the court steno-
grapher, died before transcribing even half of his 1787
pages of notes. Instead of a new trial being ordered
though, Perry's almost indecipherable scrawlings were given
to another transcriber, who happened to be the alcoholic
uncle of the prosecuting attorney's wife. The resulting
reconstructed transcript turned out to have no less than
two thousand errors or ommissions in it.[16] Nevertheless,
the California Supreme Court rejected Chessman's demands
for a new trial, and accepted the transcripts as evidence
after corrections were made. One member of the Court,
Justice Jesse W. Carter, filed a scathing dissent:

> Because...there is no adequate record upon which
> this court may review the judgments of conviction
> against the defendant, I would reverse said

judgment [and give a new trial] on that ground
alone. A reading of the majority opinion, however, convinces me that many flagrant errors
were committed during the trial which would or-
dinarily be held to be prejudicial and require
the reversal of a judgment of conviction. In
fact, the only way I can rationalize the majority
opinion is that those concurring therein feel
that a person charged with seventeen felonies
of the character of those charged against the
defendant, and who represents himself, is not
entitled to a trial in accordance with the rules
applicable to the ordinary criminal case. I
cannot subscribe to this doctrine"[17] (emphasis
added).

Undoubtedly, Judge Carter had hit the nail on the head.

The Court had been less than pleased that this convicted

criminal had rendered their job more difficult by arro-

gantly choosing to defend himself. Chessman's rights,

it was indicated, had been undercut "by reason of his own

obdurate refusal to permit counsel to represent him."[18]

Even the United States Supreme Court could not es-

cape the prejudice which accompanied the feeling that

Chessman was an amateur interfering with the law while

simply trying to delay the inevitable. Justice Douglas

wrote: "The conclusion is irresistible that Chessman's

playing a game with the courts..."[19] Over and over again,

the intimation behind the words was that Chessman's prob-

lems all stemmed from his "refusal to allow a state-ap-

pointed lawyer to represent him...," and that even "a

lawyer who entered the case by appointment at this late

stage would be utterly helpless..." because of his absence
during the initial trial.[20]

Yet Chessman did not create world-wide controversy
simply by choosing to represent himself. The most crucial
step he took was to write a book, Cell 2455 Death Row,
which was smuggled out of prison and published in 1954.
Hailed by reviewers as "an arresting addition to the annals
of crime...a dramatic and interesting book....The most remarkable portrait of a criminal career and personality
ever produced," Chessman's account of his turning to
crime became a national bestseller, and drew world-wide
attention to his case.[21] The book converted many people
to his cause. Here was a man with a paralytic mother and
a father who had committed suicide, who while in prison had
taught himself and many other inmates law, and had learned
how to represent himself in court. Eventually he would
write two other popular books and a novel. Instead of a
"thing" on Death Row, Chessman was revealed to be a living,
sensitive and intelligent human being, and he became that
much harder to kill.

On the other hand, his book further antagonized many
of his enemies. Cell 2455 Death Row was often seen as a
narrow piece of self-serving propaganda to whip up support
and sympathy. People charged with enforcing the law were

openly hostile to the fact that Chessman's book was perceived as setting him apart from the run-of-the-mill
prisoner. Goodwin Knight, governor of California in 1954,
indicated that he was closed to suggestions of clemency:
"Nobody said the law shouldn't apply to people who write
books." The state's Attorney General echoed this belief:
"There is no reason why a man who can write a book should
have an advantage..."[22] But the obvious response is that
Chessman <u>was</u> different. He had killed no one, and he had
not even kidnapped anyone in the sense of the crime that
the Little Lindbergh Law of 1933 was aiming at punishing.
In 1951, the California state legislature had even amended
the law to mitigate the severity of its penalties, that is,
at least for prisoners under sentences of life imprisonment
without parole. The Legislature neglected to change the
death penalty provision of the statute. At the time,
Chessman was the only man such a change would have bene-
fitted.[23] Chessman's supporters were not generally in-
sisting that he should go free, merely with all the questions as to the propriety of his trial, and with all the
evidence that he was capable of, and in the process of,
being rehabilitated, that he should not be executed.

    World opinion agreed. <u>Cell 2455 Death Row</u> had been
translated into twelve foreign languages to fulfill massive

demand abroad, and the reactions by 1960 were almost unani-
mously sympathetic to Chessman's plight. In Brazil, a
petition with more than 2,500,000 signatures for clemency
was collected. In Paris, during intermission at an opera,
a table was set up and more than five hundred signatures
recorded. The London Daily Herald announced that the
execution date of Chessman "...will be a day when it will
be rather unpleasant to be an American."[24] Pleaders for
Chessman's life included: The Queen of Belgium; Dr. Albert
Schweitzer; Mrs. Eleanor Roosevelt; Aldous Huxley; Pablo
Casals; and the Vatican. All told, Sweden, Italy, Brazil,
Finland, Spain, Portugal, Britain, and France (both the conservative and the communist parites) each denounced any
execution attempt on Chessman as being "cruel and unusual"
after twelve years on Death Row.[25]

In some countries no doubt, the Chessman case was a
convenient focus for anti-American sentiment. France, for
example, was not one to criticize in that it still used
capital punishment, but DeGaulle's country could hardly
resist taking a poke at embarrassed American leadership,
even with an important "Big Four" summit conference
scheduled for May 1960. That events in just one state
could put the whole of America on the defensive was surprising, but no where better demonstrated than in the weeks

just prior to President Eisenhower's good-will tour of
South America. In Brazil and Uruguay, demonstrations against
Chessman's execution were being planned to coincide with
the President's visits. On pressure from the State Department, Governor Pat Brown stayed Chessman's death for
what was to be the eighth and final time, so that the President's trip could proceed smoothly.[26]

Some reaction to this move was moderate, as evidenced
in one writer's lament about the lack of understanding that
had placed such a strain on foreign affairs. On the one
hand, opposition to the death penalty was a "civilized"
moral viewpoint, and on the other hand, insistence that
every man get a fair trial was one too. So on the basis of
these two "decent" motives, the United States was looking
bad abroad because it took almost twelve years to solve
them.[27]

Not everyone was so restrained in their response.
The attitudes of many Americans towards Chessman were
hardened by what they perceived as unwarranted foreign
interference in U.S. domestic affairs. Many politicians
were confirmed in their view that the Chessman case was a
liability better gotten rid of soon. Governor Brown, in
granting the stay, had tried to spread a little responsibility by putting a general abolition bill before the

California Assembly, but the motion was inevitably viewed as a decision on Chessman's fate. As one of his lawyers, George T. Davis, said: "Many in the legislature have favored abolition of capital punishment if taking this step won't save Chessman's life."[28] The bill was defeated in committee by an 8-7 vote.

It was the public, though, fueled by misinformation and generally sensationalist journalism, which sustained the drive for Chessman's execution. Governor Brown was inundated after the final postponement with letters which displayed as their main attributes all forms of ignorance, prejudice, and disregard for legal and human rights.[29] Brown commented that he had "...never witnessed such a display of mass hysteria, the reaction had all the earmarks of a lynch mob."[30] Though a committed abolitionist, Brown was also a politician with ambitions, who saw little gain in granting clemency to an arrogant unpopular man convicted of seventeen felonies, including sex crimes. In denying a final plea for clemency, Brown explained: "The established findings of this case...have weighed heavily in my thinking. So, too, has Chessman's failure to show contrition. His attitude has been one of steadfast arrogance and contempt for society and its laws."[31]

The public at large, administrators and officials all

over, felt that Chessman was a strictly evil man, who in
refusing to admit his guilt and in using "mere" legal
technicalities, had managed to bring the nation's system
of justice under fire. The New Republic magazine tried
to describe what it saw many people as feeling: "It is
now essential to kill him in order to revalidate our
system of justice that he has brought into disrepute by
his stratagems. He must die that we people may remain
content with our laws and our courts."[32] The New York
Times confirmed this perception: "The whole case has a
Kafkaish ring of a very evil man twisting his own misdeeds
confusingly into arguments on his own behalf, by exploiting
society's own shortcomings."[33] At no time was Chessman's
twelve year ordeal seen as anything but self-inflicted
agony. The delay was never attributed to the error of
the state, but always to Chessman's use of "mere technicalities" and "legal angles."[34]

Chessman was losing out at both ends. Among people
who did not cherish concepts of due process as inimical
to the working of the legal system, Chessman's use of
what they saw as minor procedural points was irrelevant
to the ghastly sex crimes he had committed and should be
punished for. Technicalities, after all, would not change
the nature of the evil he had done. Not surprisingly,

these same people were unconcerned that Chessman's kidnapping conviction, and thus his death sentence, hung on
nothing but a technicality of the law. On the other hand,
even people who valued a meticulous adherence to due
process in applying justice frequently failed to see any
lack of fairness in the Chessman case. Rather than look
at individual points of the law involved that had been previously used to order new trials for many other convicts,
these people tended to look at the Chessman picture as a
whole, in which twelve years of litigation must mean due
process was being adequately satisfied.

Emotional response to the Chessman controversy, however, was the rule, and rationality the exception. In
this respect, much of the newspaper journalism after the
publication of Cell 2455 Death Row was highly irresponsible,
and stoked the fire of the forces demanding Chessman's
death.[35] He was described as a "monster" and an "evil
genius," Other stories referred to the "rapist-killer"
or the "kidnap-rapist" Chessman. Of course, only kidnapper
was legally accurate, but even that conveyed the image of
a crime which Chessman did not commit, taking a victim to
hold for ransom, and the newspapers usually did not bother
to distinguish between the two.[36]

And then there was the picture of Chessman abusing

the benign properties of the judicial system in order to
save his life. The New York Times encouraged this viewpoint: "Federal judges, even while handling his appeals,
have denounced them as travesties."[37] The public was
widely led to believe that "legal loopholes" were the only
matter of substance between Chessman and the gas chamber,
and therefore, if he was not executed, it would constitute
a debacle of the law. In 1960, legal technicalities were
mostly viewed as methods for circumventing one's "just
deserts," and not as the outgrowth of inalienable human
rights, whether one was a criminal or not. Future adjudications of the Warren Court would stress the importance
of a criminal defendant's legal rights, but these landmark discussions would come too late to educate a populace
which was clamoring for Chessman's immediate execution.[38]

Newspaper reporting did Chessman perhaps the greatest
injustice in attributing Mary Meza's subsequent schizo-
phrenia to her harrowing experience at the hands of the
Red Light Bandit. In 1954, the Los Angeles Times wrote
that the girl "...became insane as a result of the indig-
nities to which she was subjected" and four years later,
the paper repeated the charge, referring to Chessman's
crimes and the "...sex attacks which put one girl into an
insane asylum."[39] Clearly this angle was too juicy for

papers to pass by, even if it was not true. Mary Meza
was ill fully five years before the incident, and was not
committed until twenty-one months later, with the Los
Angeles County psychiatric court consultant, Dr. George
Thompson, testifying that the attack was irrelevant to
the girl's present condition.[40] Later, Thompson had to
satisfy Governor Brown on this point during clemency proceedings, and wrote: "It is my opinion that this patient
was so mentally ill that her schizophrenic psychosis would
have developed regardless of any alleged attempted rape."[41]
No psychiatrist ever testified to the contrary, but the
cause and effect analysis of Meza's problems was too eminently believable for the newspapers and reading public
to think or say otherwise.

The Chessman case impassioned people, and induced in
many a complete lack of objectivity. To pinpoint the primary reason for these inflamed passions, one has to remember that the Red Light Bandit had been committing sex crimes
which were slowly spreading a net of terror and inhibition
over much of Los Angeles.[42] When Chessman was caught,
this fear was channelled into outrage at the man who could
willfully perpetrate these "unnatural" (as defined by California law) sex acts. Unlike murderers, whom society is
frequently willing to believe are insane or acting out of

control, sexual criminals of the Bandit's type are generally treated as deliberative and calculating, or at least
fully responsible for their actions. Perhaps this reaction is because many people subconsciously recognize similar sexual desires in themselves, but then repress them.
The resulting guilt at experiencing such feelings can then
be appeased by attacking someone like Chessman, who has seemingly unrestrainedly acted upon his sexual cravings. As the
late psychologist Dr. Charles Berg once wrote: "Instead of
eradicating the source of guilt feelings inside.us, if we
can find these 'wicked' tendencies in some other person,
particularly if he has given himself away, we then have a
scapegoat ready to hand. It is so much more comfortable
to exterminate...somebody else, than to suffer internally
ourselves."[43] In refusing to admit his guilt or show contrition, Chessman simply aggravated the problems for himself by trying to deny people their vicarious atonement.
Finally, in writing a book which in essence looked to en-
vironmental explanations for his turning to crime, Chessman
was not only refusing to give people a scapegoat, but was
also pinning responsibility on society itself for the
product it had turned out. People weren't ready to deal
with the guilt that recognition involved either.

    Caryl Chessman was destroyed in a wave of mass public

hysteria that derived in part from the above reasons.
When this hatred didn't directly affect the legislature
and governor in charge of Chessman's fate, the political
pressures did. Few realized or bothered to question that
politicians didn't have to buckle under to mob demand,
or that the gravity of the life and death issue involved
might transcend election and vote concerns, or the negative impact of Chessman's personality.[44] The basic issue
at stake was well expressed by one of Chessman's lawyers:
"The question at this point is not whether Chessman is
guilty or innocent. It is whether, if he inhales cyanide,
it has been done legally, and in accordance with our concepts of fair play."[45] In the atmosphere of the time, an
unbiased determination on this matter had become extremely
difficult.

Yet while many people felt that justice had been done
in ridding the world of Caryl Chessman, many others did
not, and were outraged. Americans who had not been previously overly concerned with the issue of capital punishment began to reconsider their position precisely because
the execution did not coincide with their notions of fair
play. They felt that due process had been abrogated
specifically in Chessman's case, and also that his execution after twelve years on death row served no useful

human or societal goal. Of course, these arguments had always been basic abolitionist material, but the Chessman case highlighted for people in a way no other case ever had, the injustice of the death penalty as a _reality_, rather than as an abstract possibility. Uppermost in these sentiments was a sense of Chessman's rehabilitation, or at least his potential to contribute positively to society. "Chessman was the best teacher of illiterates I ever saw," wrote Warden Duffy of San Quentin.[46]   As a New York _Herald_-_Tribune_ article eulogized: "California sentenced a young thug: it killed a man who had learned law, and probably citizenship, the hard way."[47]

To measure empirically the influence the Chessman case had on capital punishment related developments of the Sixties is, of course, impossible, but its impact nevertheless should not be underrated. For some people, there seemed to be a direct cause and effect relationship between Chessman's execution and their support for abolition. Douglas Lyons, eleven years old in 1960, was one such person. A decade later he would be the head of C.A.L.M. (Citizens Against Legalized Murder), an organization very influential in the eventual halting of executions in America by 1968.[48] Even if for other people, the Chessman case wasn't so decisive a factor in their thinking, it nevertheless brought

the issue of capital punishment to the forefront of their
consciousness, and made the death penalty in America a
legitimate political issue of controversy.[49]

The cry for vengeance which led to Chessman's ultimate destruction was particularly disconcerting to these
Americans. Neither deterrence nor protection of society
arguments could reasonably be said to be involved in a
case which took twelve years to resolve and saw its subject well on the road to reform. The need to kill Caryl
Chessman was therefore stripped down to its essential
motivation: the fulfillment of retributive urges. This
recognition then posed the issue of capital punishment
as primarily a moral judgment as to whether a revenge
impulse alone is a worthy rationale for punishment. A
1960 Gallup poll on capital punishment finding that "...a
considerable proportion of the arguments on both sides
are in religious terms" confirms that the appropriateness
of vengeance was becoming a prevalent concern.[50]

In Great Britain, the discovery that an innocent man,
Timothy Evans, was hung in 1950 is generally credited with
spurring the abolition of capital punishment in that
country.[51] It is not unreasonable to suggest the Chessman case as a parallel. Even if he was guilty of being
the Red Light Bandit (of which there is considerable doubt)

a growing consensus arose that in both a legal and a
moral sense, Caryl Chessman should not have been destroyed.
Conscience-stricken people began to support or work for
the abolition of capital punishment as a result.

The Education of a Populace

The ending of executions in America after 1967 was
primarily the result of legal machinations in the courts
(see Chapter Four) but the complete story of capital
punishment cannot be told within such a narrow focus.
The social climate of the day deserves mention because on
the whole, it tended to heighten people's sensitivity to
anti-capital punishment arguments. Public opinion was
shifting, governors were not signing execution warrants,
abolition bills were being considered and passed by legislatures, and prestigious civil rights organizations, like
the NAACP's Legal Defense Fund and the American Civil Liberties Union (ACLU) were adopting the abolition of capital
punishment as their cause. Courts do not operate in a
political vacuum, and their increasing receptivity to constitutional arguments against the death penalty must be
considered in light of the above trends. Nevertheless,
except for the last few months of Chessman's struggle to
avoid the San Quentin gas chamber, capital punishment simply
did not attract that much attention as an issue. The

nation's movement towards an anti-capital punishment pos-
ture during the Sixties, therefore, calls for an explanation
in terms of the country's developing political consciousness.
In this sense, the death penalty was a collateral issue for
many Americans, on which opinions were modified in order to
conform to new knowledge, experience, or perceptions.

The problem for the historian then becomes one of explaining patterns in public opinion in terms of contemporary events. Specifically, one would hope to determine
the causes for the downward trend in support for capital
punishment that persisted through 1966. In order to avoid
completely surrendering to the realm of speculation, it
will be useful first to set down a few distinctions as to
the types of opinion on capital punishment, and how these
beliefs might be formed. Simply put, support for the death
penalty is predicated on either pragmatic and utilitarian
aspects of the punishment, a perceived moral good (e.g. retri
bution) which is furthered by the punishment, or some com-
bination of these two factors. In turn, these beliefs can
be affected or altered basically on two levels: societal
conditioning, or individual conditioning, either of which
might change the context or moral setting of the belief.
This dichotomy will become clearer with an example.

On the individual level, violence experienced as a
child within a family might be crucial in the determination

of one's willingness to punish criminals depending upon
the amount of internalization of the experienced violence
occurs. In other words, violence could be "taught" within
the family as an acceptable form of expression, problem
solving, or controlling behavior, and be passed on from
generation to generation in this method without any particular external influences.[52] (see appendix B) Though
much more could be said about this topic, it is really
a sociological matter beyond the scope of this study.

The equivalent on a societal level of condoning violence is war, and it is on this level of analysis that history can be of greater use. War can be viewed as weakening
the principle of the sanctity of life and as legitimizing
the use of violence in general. Thus one might expect
support for the death penalty to be higher in a country
waging war. In examining what America stood for in the
early Sixties, and what the public issues of concern were,
one can get a greater understanding of the pressures and
forces which would induce a modification of people's views
on capital punishment. The Vietnam War is a logical
starting point.

The war in Indochina was not typical of American wars.
First, the United States was essentially involving itself
in someone else's civil war. Second, its grisly aspects

were being revealed in meticulous detail through the
television medium. Third, the United States was losing,
and not achieving its goals. These factors set the stage
for protesting American involvement, and the argument can
be made that by late 1965 and early 1966, when these negative aspects first began to receive attention, the Vietnam
War was teaching the American public the opposite of
previous wars' experience. Namely, violence was not an
effective means to an end, was not anything to glorify,
and was not necessarily justified whenever the government
said so. Polls reveal that the first major public weakenin
of support for the War roughly coincided with the erosion o
support for the death penalty.[53]

	"Do you approve or disapprove of the way President Johnson is handling the situation in Vietnam?"				
	Dec.1965	Mar.1966	May 1966	Sept.1966	July 1967
Approve:	56%	50%	47%	43%	33%
Disapprove:	26%	33%	35%	40%	52%

The evidence suggests therefore, that the war increased
many people's resistance to accepting blandly governmental
justifications for killing, and also that it served to
sharpen many people's moral sensitivity to killing in
general. Insofar as these lessons were applied to capital
punishment, opposition to executions grew also.

It is also worth speculating on the effect the Civil
Rights movement of the early Sixties had on support for the
death penalty. Previously accepted and settled social
arrangements between races began to fall apart, as the blacks
demanded and expected political, economic, and eventually
social equality. The Civil Rights Act of 1964, the Voting
Rights Act of 1965 and the Affirmative Action programs
were the Johnson administration's attempt to incorporate
equal opportunity for the black population into United
States law. This process necessitated the re-examination
in general of a societal structure and body of law which
served to subjugate one class under another. Empirical
evidence as to the discriminatory nature of the death
penalty began to be impressively compiled only during
this period (see Chapter Two). Capital punishment then became a casualty of the Civil Rights movement to the extent it spurred recognition of the death penalty as one
instrument of repression of blacks and minorities.

Most importantly, the N.A.A.C.P.'s Legal Defense
Fund realized that the death penalty was intimately con-
nected with the question of civil rights, and decided
that it was necessary to end the use of capital punishment.
As one Fund lawyer wrote," [the LDF] came to believe that
it was impossible to separate racism from the death

penalty; that the only remedy for discrimination was to ensure that the opportunity to execute blacks simply did not arise."[54] For the LDF, the abolition of capital punishment would form an integral part of the black man's fight to gain equality in America.

The Civil Rights movement also had a secondary, but nonetheless crucial effect on the halting of executions, and that was the willingness to use litigation to gain the desired end. The segregation battle in Little Rock, Arkansas had quite literally forced the LDF to go to court to try to win its battle against discrimination, and the Supreme Court had been surprisingly receptive to this approach.[55] For groups like the blacks, without political power or great lobbying capabilities, reform through the judiciary was highly attractive. The court system was viewed as being relatively insulated from the intolerance of public opinion, and therefore a better forum for the protection of minority rights than the legislature. Thus with the encouragement of the dissent filed by Justices Goldberg, Douglas, and Brennan in the aforementioned Rudolph v. Alabama case (see p.71), the LDF was ready to take its case against capital punishment to the courts. Without a coordinated civil rights movement in America, it is doubtful that such litigation ever would have taken place.

The civil rights agitation also marked the rise of
another phenomenon endemic to the Sixties, and that was
the development of a theory of environmentalism as the
root of crime and unrest. The Sixties forced people to
realize that the American dream had not worked: blacks
were discontented, women were dissatisfied, and the youth
were rebelling. The pride of America, its prosperity,
military power, and technological powers, had been unable
to achieve a unanimity of spirit. As protests, sit-ins
and ghetto riots began to surface, the United States was
forced to undergo an introspection whose only conclusion
could be that the system and style of governing accepted
since post-World War II had failed dramatically for substantial segments of the population. This comprehension
paved the way for the recognition of alternative goals
for government, a fact perhaps best reflected in growing
public and congressional acceptance of Lyndon Johnson's
"great society" program.[56]

In the meantime, people began to sympathize with
the impulses which turned a person to crime and anti-social behavior. It was hard to look at a Watts or South
Bronx without acknowledging that powerful conditioning
forces were at work which America had created and tolerated.

In a 1964 Gallup poll, for example, 51% of the respondents
believed the causes of crime in some fashion to be en-
vironmentally related (parents, home life to blame 41%;
unemployment 5%; lack of education 5%), while only 27%
looked to the individual criminals as responsible (need
for tougher law enforcement 18%; lack of respect for the
law 9%).[57] Accordingly, the inclination to deal with
crime by severe punishment had to be reconsidered. It was
inconsistent to fight a "war against poverty" to deal with
anti-social behavior on the one hand, while continuing to
mete out severe punishments on the other. If society
was partly responsible for producing the misfits and hostile personalities brought before the courts, how could
it justify slaughtering them in death chambers? Capital
punishment would then simply constitute a repression of
guilt and an abdication of responsibility. By imprisoning
dangerous criminals, society could still protect itself,
but simultaneously work to eradicate the roots of the
criminal mentality.[58]

The Two Faces of Reform

It would be ingenuous to contend that people ferv-
ently believed in and supported these theories. Rather,
it was more likely that people were simply willing to

accept them for the time being, due to a variety of variables at work. Presidential and governmental leadership
was one such factor. The Johnson administration tended
to put its full weight behind the "great society" program
and the goals it represented. LBJ was intent upon eliminating "blights" on American history, and this effort
had an effect, if only to force America to realize that
such "blights" did, in fact, exist. Nor should one under-
estimate the tendency for people to align their opinions
with those of their leaders. Thus, Ramsey Clark's advo-
cating the abolition of federal death penalty statutes
probably was influential to a degree, though not as much
as it could have been if the Johnson administration had
not lost a great deal of its credibility because of Vietnam.[59]

Similarly, it's worth mentioning that people frequently prefer to align their opinions to their own self-
image. The major issues of the Sixties, Vietnam and Civil
Rights, eventually created a national consensus which was
"liberal" or left of center on a political continuum. It
would be surprising if at least some people didn't modify
their position on capital punishment (perhaps an irrelevant controversy to them) simply to conform to their
political identification on Vietnam and Civil Rights.
In this sense the polls might express a popular support

for the abolition of capital punishment that was wider
than it was deep.[60] Thus the resolution to most people's
satisfaction of the War and the Civil Rights issue might
help to explain the considerable erosion of support
for abolition experienced in the late Sixties and early
Seventies.

The actual state of executions in America is also
important in evaluating the significance of public opinion
on capital punishment. As long as executions are actually
taking place, there will always be a significant number
of people opposed to the death penalty simply because the
reality of its imposition is revolting to them. Yet if
executions are halted, as they were by 1968, the objection
to the idea of capital punishment may be eliminated, at
least until the executions are resumed. In other words,
it is much easier to accept capital punishment in theory
than in practice.[61] As an example, one team of researchers
discovered that "although many people endorsed capital pun-
isment at the general level, the degree of support for it
dropped considerably when they were asked a more precise
question about how they would behave if serving on a jury."[6]
If executions are not occuring, support for abolition is
predicted on much more abstract concepts, such as fairer
justice, which may not be convincing in the face of more

concrete arguments for the death penalty, such as safer
streets, or less crime. In this sense, increased support
for capital punishment after 1967 may simply be a symbolic
attitude, reflecting people's desire for more law and order,
or less crime. Yet recommence executions, and it is probable that support for capital punishment will tail off.

Reinforcing this theory is the fact that the early
Sixties, up until about 1967, was a period of relative
economic prosperity and low crime rates. A high rate of
growth for the nation seemed to promise more of everything
for everyone. If any environment is conducive to toler-
ance and social experimentation, it is one displaying
these characteristics. Yet by late 1967, fully 60% of the
country was saying the major problem they faced as individuals was the high cost of living.[63] The nation was
experiencing its greatest inflation rates of the decade,
and unemployment was growing.[64] Such conditions inevitably
aggravate the crime rate and increase public perceptions
of crime as a problem. Throughout the Sixties, for example,
in response to the question "what do you think is the most
important problem facing this country today?" no more
than 4% of the public had ever answered "crime." Yet
by May 1968, all of a sudden 15% were citing crime, and
one month later the figure had skyrocketed to 29%.[65]

A rising crime rate, in that it increases one's fear
of victimization, invariably limits humanitarian impulses,
undermines satisfaction or patience with social reforms,
and enhances the urge to react with stronger punitive
measures. As one sociological study reported: "Public
support for severe penal sanctions derives largely from
public perception of a rising tide of criminal violence,
whether or not that violence in fact is rising and whether
or not it is susceptible to deterrence or prevention by
punitive sanctions."[66] It should come as no surprise
then, that support for the death penalty began to increase
by 1968 (and continues to do so today).[67]

	"Are you in favor of the death penalty for people convicted of murder?"				
	1966	1969	1971	1972	1976
Yes:	42	51	49	57	65
No:	47	40	40	32	28

The absence of capital punishment was blamed for the
increase in murders, and its reintroduction was looked
forward to as a virtual panacea. Senator McClellan,
for example, in introducing the death penalty bill S1401,
commented: "The last execution in this country took place

in 1967... In the five years between 1967 and 1971, the
number of murders in this country rose 61%....Can
anyone argue that this was a mere coincidence?"[68] Well
of course they can. The same statistics the Senator
used show that the rate for violent crimes not punishable by death rose even more: 80% (larceny rose 99%).[69]
But the fact that the Senator was egregiously misleading
his   listeners is not really the point. Rather, it is
important to see the appeal capital punishment regained
as soon as conditions in the country were seen as less
favorable to social experimentation. As a New York Times
editorial lamented, "The death penalty once again ranks
high as an antidote to what President Nixon has denounced
as 'permissiveness'..."[70] In this sense, advocacy of
capital punishment may be related more to people's impatience with the complexities of liberalism, higher crime
rates, and a seemingly ineffective court system, than
to any real feeling that the death penalty will solve
anything.[71]

The symbolic value of attitudes on the death penalty
as a measure of a soft or hard line stand on social issues
should not be underemphasized. The early Sixties en-
compassed an unprecedented upheaval in America's outlook

on the society it had created. The United States had
given birth to a huge revolution of expectations, and
was quickly confronted with its own inability to fulfill it. But the response during the first and middle
half of the decade was a shift towards innovation and a
heavy emphasis on social reform, and partly as a result,
support for capital punishment diminished. Yet the process cut both ways. While the demonstrations, the riots,
the Civil Rights Acts, the campus uprisings and the Vietnam War fueled the fires of change, they also prepared
the way for a conservative backlash in which faith in
the efficacy of social reform disappeared in a wave of
impatience and fear, to be replaced by a tactic of
keeping the lid on social discontent through "law and
order." It was not so easy to undo what had already
started, however. Although support for the death penalty
firmed considerably in the late Sixties, a strategy of
litigation for challenging capital punishment in the
courts had previously emerged, gained independent force,
and escaped unscathed. Ultimately this legal approach
would upset every death penalty statute in America.

CHAPTER FOUR

        From the beginning, a procession of the poor,
    the weak, the unfit, have gone through our jails and
    prisons to their deaths. They have been victims.
    Crime and poverty and ignorance have always gone
    hand in hand. When our lawmakers realize this,
    they will stop legislating more punishment and
    go after the causes.
                                        Clarence Darrow

    In the early Sixties, capital punishment was a sec-

ondary issue for the Legal Defense Fund. The civil rights

fight quite naturally was the main concern of an organ-

ization dedicated to the "advancement of colored people."[1]

The LDF's time and money was already spread thin in handling

the numerous protests and litigation arising out of the

integration cases that the Justice Department had been lax

in enforcing. Capital punishment cases were dealt with

solely on a one by one basis, with sentences being challenged

on procedural errors, such as blacks being excluded from

juries or coercive police tactics being used to extract

confessions. Although in 1961 lawyer Gerald Gottlieb

had suggested that capital punishment might be unconstitu-

tional under the Eighth Amendment's clause forbidding

"cruel and unusual" punishment, no one particularly thought

that challenging the broader legality of the death penalty

was an approach which stood a chance for success in the

courts.[2]

The Development of a Strategy

As indicated in the previous chapter, the LDF soon
began to realize that capital punishment was relevant to
the organization's aims. The mounting evidence of discrimination against blacks in capital sentencing for rape
was just beginning to confirm what observation had always
suggested. Here was an area where lawyers' knowledge and
a strategy of litigation might best be put to use. The
glory days of the civil rights movement were fading, and
were being replaced by a new emphasis on battles and protests in the streets, and on urban riots. As LDF member
Michael Meltsner explained, "no one feels so irrelevant as
a lawyer in a shoot-out."[3]

A quick glance at some Death Rows in the South highlighted the need condemned men had for an organization to
represent their interests. In Florida, for example, LDF
executive director Jack Greenberg explained that of the
men whose appeals had been denied, "all were indigent --
half without counsel, half with volunteers. The mean intel-
ligence level was considerably below normal."[4] Eventually
LDF lawyers saw themselves as morally committed to save
anyone they could, regardless of skin color, and not merely

to concern themselves with discrimination in rape cases.
As Greenberg asserted:

> One cannot ignore the prejudices, not merely
> racial, that bring a jury to select this man and
> not another for death -- indeed, to select any man
> for death for any crime.... It was not adequate
> to assert [claims] on behalf of some defendants
> and ignore other defendants in the hope that they
> would receive the benefit of a new rule announced
> at a later date.5

If the legal techniques were available, the LDF could not
comfortably choose to try to save some men, while letting
others die. Inequity was intrinsic to capital punishment,
and it seemed clear that the only way to resolve the problem was to eliminate the form of punishment. No doubt
subtle and invidious discrimination permeated the whole
legal system, but at least, the LDF reasoned, men should
not die as a result. Their attack quickly became one
against all applications of the death penalty.

At first, the LDF's commitment to their clients involved getting stays of execution and keeping condemned
men alive in any legal fashion possible, so that they
would be around to benefit from any new courtroom developments. Eventually, halting all executions became a goal
in itself, aimed at shifting the legal and moral pressures
onto those who would restart the implementation of capital
punishment. Fund lawyer Anthony Amsterdam explained the

idea behind this moratorium approach:

> The main difficulty we have been faced with is
> this argument that capital punishment is still needed
> in our society as retribution against the worst of-
> fenders, as a preventive of crime, as a way of bring-
> ing about greater morality. It's a ridiculous argument
> with absolutely nothing to back it up, but it's so
> emotional and so deeply ingrained in our society
> that it's hard to get rid of it. But if we could
> actually stop the executions, establish this condi-
> tion that so many people are afraid of, and then
> show that the country was not falling apart because
> of it, then we could stop the judges from thinking
> along the lines of this emotional argument.
> Once we stopped the executions, the courts would
> then have to face the awful reality that a decision in
> favor of capital punishment would start the blood-
> bath again.[6]

The first problem to confront, however, was the halting

of all executions.

Amsterdam was the man to whom the LDF organization

turned in order to achieve this goal. His brilliance and

powers of persuasion in oral argument were reknowned, and

even his ideological opponents begrudgingly acknowledged

his talents: "I disagree with what he says, but I sure

as hell admire the skill with which he says it."[7] The

story goes that one federal judge was particularly annoyed

with Amsterdam's citation from memory of some obscure case,

and sent his clerk to the law library to look it up. The

case was nowhere to be found, and the judge antagonistic-

ally confronted Amsterdam with this fact. Amsterdam, withou

missing a beat, replied that the volume of cases must have been misbound. It was.[8]

Amsterdam, along with Greenberg, Meltsner, and a host of LDF lawyers, would eventually put in back-breaking hours in order to stop the executions and challenge the constitutionality of capital punishment. Even if the latter goal was unachievable, a moratorium, and therefore a de facto abolition of capital punishment, was promising in that the legal system paved the way for endless litigation, and no one could be executed if an appeal concerning him was still pending. Although the legal staff available was small and stretched to the limit of its resources, the Fund was not alone in its fight. Governors, judges and juries in the early Sixties were showing an increased reluctance to send men to their deaths, so that the number of appeals the Fund had to handle was manageable.

Events soon forced the Fund lawyers to work quicker than they wished. The 1965 elections had seen Ronald Reagan and Claude Kirk, Jr. gain office as Governors of California and Florida respectively, and soon afterwards, both men began to sign wholesale death warrants for condemned inmates. The Death Row populations of these two states were the largest in the country, and the prospect of keeping tabs on each man's status and getting stays of execution where necessary

seemed unworkable for the small LDF staff.[9] Drastic action
would be needed if the mid Sixties lull in the execution
rate was to be maintained.

In Florida, a novel lawsuit was worked out with the
aid of the state's ACLU affiliate chairman, Tobias Simon. A
class action suit was filed on the premise that if there
was something unconstitutional about the state's administration of capital punishment, then the prisoners on Death
Row represented a class of persons who were legally similarly
situated, and their constitutional objections to the death
penalty could all be resolved in one proceeding.[10] Although
class action suits were a common legal device in civil cases,
they had never worked successfully to challenge the sentences of all criminals who might benefit from a decision.
As Meltsner explained: "Lawyers always assumed that each
convicted criminal had to present a claim that he was
entitled to release, a new trial, or a different sentence
individually, in a separate proceeding."[11] Nevertheless, on
April 13, 1967, District Judge William McRae, Jr. responded
by ordering a temporary stay on all executions in Florida,
until the merits of a class action could be determined. In
California, in reaction to a similar suit, and with McRae's
example before him, Judge Robert Peckham acted similarly,
and on July 5, 1967, also issued an injunction.[12] The Fund

lawyers now had the extra time they needed. At least until
a test case challenging the constitutionality of capital
punishment had been heard and adjudicated, it was unlikely
that any further executions in California and Florida would
be held.

The class action stays were very precarious, however,
and the Fund worked hard to discourage their being filed
in other states where they were not an absolute necessity,
for fear of adversely affecting the California and Florida
rulings. Greenberg explicitly warned ACLU legal director
Melvin Wulf that they should "avoid, if possible, setting up the
Florida and California victories, tenuous as they are, as
targets to shoot down. It may be premature...to do anything in other jurisdictions before the California and
Florida cases jell."[13] Amsterdam urged equal caution in
writing to ACLU lawyer William Friedlander: "I would...
approach the thought of a class suit in the way in which
porcupines are said to make love -- very gingerly."[14] The
result was that little changed in the other thirty states
with inmates on death row. The Fund still had to find out
when executions were scheduled, and then find lawyers in the
area who would be willing to file for individual last-minute
stays.

To facilitate and standardize this process the Fund

issued and distributed a collection of legal briefs,
petitions and applications which detailed the apposite
constitutional arguments against the death penalty and outlined the proper procedure for getting a stay of execution.
Entitled "Documents for Proceeding in Federal Habeas Corpus
in a Capital Case in which Execution is Imminent," this
batch of papers appropriately became known as the "death-
kit."[15]

The LDF was the acknowledged leader by this time of
what had become a national movement to gain judicial
abolition of capital punishment. The limited size of the
Fund's staff and operating budget however, (despite a hefty
one million dollar Ford Foundation grant in mid- 1967)[16]
forced it to delegate responsibility wherever possible.
Nonetheless, the LDF kept a tight rein on the legal issues
it considered relevant to the abolition strategy. It
wished to restrain uninformed or careless attorneys from
going into court to save a client with ill-conceived frontal
attacks on the constitutionality of the death penalty. Such
actions could at best only serve to prejudice state and
federal judges as to the seriousness of the abolition
movement, and at worst, conceivably render future and well-
argued LDF challenges moot.

In pursuit of this aim, the Fund held a national

conference in mid-1968 to outline, in supplementation of
the "death-kit," the methods for impeding executions.
During the conference, the LDF indicated that it wanted to
concentrate solely on its legal campaign, and not on educ-
ating the legislatures or the populace at large. The Fund
was interested in community action only to the extent that
it kept attorneys informed from state to state of Death
Row inmates' status. This view of the Fund's role tended to
reinforce a natural division of labor which was already
underway between the LDF and the ACLU.[17]

The ACLU, faced with the problem of correlating all
of its affiliates' opinions before establishing national
policy, was not operating at its most efficient level in
coordinating the legal attack on capital punishment. It
had been unable to declare officially its opposition to the
death penalty until June 1965 because of dissent internally
as to whether capital punishment posed a civil liberties
issue.[18] Furthermore, the independent nature of some of
the affiliates rendered the ACLU somewhat unreliable as
an ally. In the California class action, for example,
LDF attorney Leroy Clark was rebuffed when he asked the
North California ACLU and its chairman, Marshall Krause, to
join the case as co-sponsor. One ACLU member tried to explain the nature of the problem: "Perhaps the diffidence

of Marshall Krause and the ACLU of North California to
join the NAACP Legal Defense Fund challenge in that state
relates to the fact that the North California affiliate
disagrees, I believe, with the national statement on capital
punishment."[19]   Clearly this lack of unanimity was no way
to run an unprecedented and complex legal campaign against
the death penalty. The LDF, with its small core of dedicated attorneys, was better suited to directing a cohesive
and consistent attack. Consequently, the ACLU began a
heightened emphasis on the community education aspect of the
death penalty campaign, but continued to lend its name,
prestige, and many of its lawyers in support of the LDF
(usually as amicus curiae) where it was appropriate and
could be worked out.[20]

The Issues

During the national conference, Amsterdam had stressed
to the attendees that it would probably be more effective
"to attack the death penalty collaterally than by a head-on
challenge to its constitutionality."[21]   Essentially this
instruction meant that the "Due Process" and "Equal Protection"
of the Laws" clauses of the Fourteenth Amendment were the
best method for attacking capital punishment in the courts.
The Supreme Court had recently been interpreting the Amendment

dynamically to expand the scope of criminal defendants'
rights,[22] so it was thought that there were several
arguments to which the nine Justices might be receptive.[23]
The first would be to show racial discrimination in the application of capital punishment, especially for the rape of
white women by blacks. The evidence was strong, but the
LDF would have to convince the Court that other factors
did not account for the sentencing discrepencies between
the races. The potential for abusing the judicial system
through the interpretation of statistics was great, and
the Court was still dealing with criticism of its use of un-
confirmed sociological evidence in the 1954 desegregation
ruling.[24]

The second mode of attack would focus on the practice
of trying capital cases with what were often referred to as
"death qualified" juries. In impanelling a jury for a
capital case, a prosecutor was allowed to reject outright a
juror who expressed any reservations or scruples about imposing the death penalty. He did not have to probe further
as to whether or not a juror might be willing to consider
the death penalty in the particular case. The Fund contended
that this process was unconstitutional for several reasons:
1. it created a "hanging jury" which in passing sentence
would be more inclined to give death; 2. it created a

"conviction prone" jury to the extent that persons favoring the death penalty were more likely to have tough "law and order"stances and be less inclined to acquit a marginally guilty defendant; 3. a jury so selected could not be considered "trial by one's peers." Indeed, if more than forty percent of the country was against capital punishment, such a jury would not be representative of any community.

A third approach to challenging the constitutionality of capital punishment on a procedural basis would be to attack the determination of both a defendant's guilt and sentence in one trial. This so-called "single verdict" practice was the standard fare in all but five of the states with death penalty statutes, and seemed to impose a heavy cost on a defendant's Fifth Amendment rights. The problem was one of trying to present evidence which might incline a jury towards leniency in sentencing without prejudicing one's chance for a "not guilty" verdict. If a defendant waived his Fifth Amendment right and took the witness stand, his past misconduct and convictions could be brought out in cross-examination and influence a jury's guilt determination. Yet if he refused to risk this possibility, a defendant had no other method for presenting mitigating circumstances unrelated to the question of guilt. The LDF argued that this dilemma created an unconstitutiona

tension between a defendant's Fifth Amendment right against
self-incrimination and his right to present evidence relevant to intelligent sentencing.

The Fund's final procedural argument against capital
punishment would be the contention that it was unconstitutional
to leave a life and death decision to the unfettered discretion of a jury. When most states had decided to replace
mandatory sentencing with discretionary sentencing around
the turn of the century, they had prescribed absolutely no
standards for a jury to follow in determining whether a
defendant should be imprisoned or executed. In that manner,
the legislatures had hoped, the problem of "jury nullification" would be eliminated. Yet this procedure essentially
amounted to an abdication by the state assemblies as to
explaining the state and penological policy ends of retaining
capital punishment. The result, the LDF argued, was that
juries were free to pass judgment depending entirely on
their own perceptions, prejudices, and biases. Unlike in
negligence cases, for example, the jury was given no body
of law which it then was supposed to apply. Since juries
inevitably varied depending upon the individuals who com-
posed them, there was no assurance that one defendant would
be sentenced on a basis even vaguely resembling that
applied to another. True, this argument applied to most

criminal proceedings, but it was a recognized tenet of constitutional law that due process requirements became stricter
as the interests at stake increased. To permit citizens to
be arbitrarily, perhaps discriminatorily, sentenced to death
due to a lack of regularized procedure, the LDF concluded,
was constitutionally impermissible.

Generally, the LDF did not consider a frontal attack
on capital punishment being unconstitutional under the
Eighth Amendment's clause forbidding "cruel and unusual"
punishment as rating a high chance of success. Amsterdam
had specifically emphasized "the limited value of the
Eighth Amendment as a legal argument" during the LDF
national conference.[25] First of all, the constitution
specifically assumed the legitimacy of capital punishment
in the Fifth and Fourteenth Amendments.[26] Although the Fifth
Amendment also seemed to indicate the acceptance in 1791 of
corporal punishment, which no one would argue was permissible in the twentieth century, the Supreme Court had
shown great reluctance to overturn any legislatively approved punishments as "cruel and unusual." Historically, the
adoption of the Eighth Amendment was viewed as intending
simply to prohibit barbaric treatment or punishment unauth-
orized by law. In 1890, for example, the Court in deciding
whether New York State could use electrocution to execute

Willie Kemmler, had declared that the Eighth Amendment only
proscribed "burning at the stake, crucifixion, breaking on
the wheel, or the like."[27] In a 1947 case, the Court refused to overturn the sentence of a man who had survived
the first attempt to execute him, and was to be strapped into
the chair for a second time. The majority opinion relied on
the fact that an accident had caused the problem, and that
it was not the intent of the State to impose a cruel death.[28]
These opinions effectively seemed to consign the Eighth
Amendment to dead law. Any punishment which might be cruel
and unusual under these rulings had been long abandoned, and
no one was likely to advocate a return to maiming or cutting
off limbs.

More recent opinions had expanded the scope of the
Eighth Amendment somewhat, but still left questions un-
answered as to its meaning. The 1958 case of Trop v. Dulles[29]
had held that stripping a native born American of his citizenship upon conviction of desertion in wartime constituted
"cruel and unusual" punishment. Chief Justice Warren wrote
for the Court: "The Amendment must draw its meaning from
the evolving standards of decency that mark the progress
of a maturing society....The basic concept underlying the
[Eighth Amendment] is nothing less than the dignity of man."[30]
(emphasis added). Yet at the same time, the Chief Justice
added that capital punishment was still widely accepted

and by no means could be considered constitutionally cruel and unusual.

A 1962 adjudication, Robinson v. California,[31] struck down a California statute punishing addiction to narcotics with a ninety day to one year sentence on the basis that it was "cruel and unusual" to "make illness a crime." Of course, no one was denying that the actions were criminal for which capital punishment was invoked, but the Robinson decision, in citing Trop, was significant in two areas: 1. i confirmed that changing standards and increased knowledge were factors in interpreting the Eighth Amendment; 2. it established beyond doubt that the Eighth Amendment was applicable to the states through the Due Process Clause of the Fourteenth Amendment.[32] All the same, the Fund preferre not to rely too heavily on the Eighth Amendment as the tool with which to attack capital punishment. Considering the fact that more than forty states and the Federal Government maintained capital punishment for one crime or another, it was hard to argue convincingly that the death penalty offended "evolving standards of decency."

The Cases

The first major indication that the Supreme Court was willing to tighten up the procedure by which the death penalty was administered came in the 1968 case of U.S. v. Jackson.[33] The Court ruled the Federal Kidnapping Act unconstitutional as "imposing an impermissible burden upon an accused's exercise of his Fifth Amendment right not to plead guilty and his Sixth Amendment right to demand a jury trial."[34] The problem was that the law only extended the threat of the death penalty to defendants who pleaded not guilty and went to trial. A defendant who pleaded guilty could not receive a death sentence, and the Court ruled that this choice was too heavy an incentive to waive one's right to a jury trial. The LDF was pleased with the decision because not only did it save many prisoners from execution and therefore solidify the tenuous moratorium in effect since Louis José Monge had been gassed in Colorado on June 2, 1967, but because it also seemed to acknowledge that death was a quantifiably different penalty from any form of imprisonment. This recognition was the foot in a door the LDF was going to push wide open.

A more significant victory for the Fund lawyers came later in 1968 in the case of Witherspoon v. Illinois,[35] concerning the matter of "death qualified" juries. Illinois law permitted the challenging of any juror who stated that "he has conscientious scruples against capital punishment," and in this particular trial, almost half the venire of

prospective jurors had been excused (47 out of 96).[36] The
trial judge had actually been recorded as saying "let's get
these conscientious objectors out of the way, without wast-
ing any time on them."[37] The Supreme Court ruled that such
a jury could not be impartial in selecting a punishment. The
Court did not go so far as to accept the LDF's argument that
this jury was also "prosecution prone," however, citing a
lack of evidence on this point.[38] Only the choosing of
punishment could be considered biased, not the determination
of guilt. Furthermore, states could still exclude jurors
who declared that they would never impose the death penalty,
or at least not in the particular case. All the ruling
required prosecutors and judges to do was to delve a little
deeper into the psyches of veniremen who expressed ambiguous sentiments about the death penalty and to determine
whether they could impose a death sentence.

Nevertheless, it seemed conceivable that the Witherspoon
ruling would have the practical effect of abolishing capital
punishment in the United States. Nearly all Death Row
inmates appeared to have some sort of a claim to resentencing under the Witherspoon verdict, and new juries structured
to satisfy the decision's requirements would probably be
less inclined to impose death. In reality this hope did not
work out, as many lower courts interpreted Witherspoon

narrowly or wrongly, and as many new penalty hearings
reaffirmed prisoners' previous death sentences.[39]   Yet
the Witherspoon ruling indicated that the Court was sensitive to flaws in the process which condemned men to death,
and was not afraid to act accordingly. For the LDF
lawyers, postponement of executions became easier to get,
and the moratorium began to solidify.

The 1969 case of Boykin v. Alabama,[40] however, confirmed what the Fund already feared about the usefulness
of the Eighth Amendment. Boykin was arrested on five robbery counts, and plead guilty to each of them. The less
than sympathetic jury promptly returned five death sentences,
as permitted by Alabama law. The LDF decided to handle
Boykin's appeal, and presented three issues to the Court:
1. death for robbery constituted cruel and unusual punishment; 2. the lack of sentencing standards was unconstitutional;
3. Boykin did not make his guilty plea with the knowledge
that it subjected him to the chance of electrocution. The
Supreme Court, however, did not rule on the petitioner's
raising of the first two issues, and overturned Boykin's
sentences on the narrowest possible grounds: that he did
not voluntarily and understandingly enter his guilty plea.
It was widely felt that this decision did not portend a
particularly active role for the Eighth Amendment. Five

death sentences for robbery was about as disproportionate
and cruel a sentence as the Court could ever hope to see.
Fund lawyers were agreed that the constitutionality of the
death penalty would probably rise or fall on the Fourteenth
Amendment.[41]

One of the earliest capital cases the LDF had entered
was on behalf of William Maxwell, a black rapist sentenced
to death in Arkansas. The Fund had initially sought to
prove racial discrimination in Arkansas rape sentencing,
but the lower courts had made it clear that statistics
formed a dubious foundation for any such adjudication.[42] It
was hard to expect a court to make a ruling which would
indict hundreds of past executions as being based on discrimination. On appeal to the Supreme Court, the Fund
persisted with the discrimination argument, but also raised
the unlimited jury discretion and the single verdict questions, and the Court granted _certiorari_ on these latter
two issues.[43] Even if discrimination was not to be considered
the LDF was pleased to have a test case which would resolve
these two crucial matters.

Or would it? Before _Maxwell_ was decided, Associate
Justice Abe Fortas was forced from the Court by a conflict of
interest controversy, and Chief Justice Earl Warren retired. The two Nixon replacements, Harry Blackmun and

Warren Burger, complicated the logistics of the case.
Blackmun had ruled on the Maxwell suit in the Circuit Court
of Appeals and therefore had to disqualify himself. Burger,
on the other hand, altered the ideological orientation of
the Court so that the discretion and single verdict issues
now would be left unresolved by a four to four vote.[44] The
Witherspoon decision gave the Justices a way out. Although
Amsterdam argued that it was "plain that disposition of
petitioner's case on Witherspoon grounds would not render
his other claims moot,"[45] the Court disagreed, and disposed
of Maxwell's appeal on the basis that he had been sentenced
by a death qualified jury. As abolitionists groaned in
frustration, however, the Court announced it was granting
review in two cases, McGautha v. California and Crampton v.
Ohio[46] on the same undecided Maxwell issues of standardless
sentencing and single verdict trials.

The LDF was not overjoyed with this choice of cases.
Dennis McGautha had committed a vicious homicide during a
robbery in California. California provided for a bifurcated
trial, so McGautha's appeal only raised the standards issue, yet in this particular instance, the jury's discretion
had undeniably functioned reasonably. McGautha had a long
record of past convictions and was sentenced to death. A
confederate in the robbery was a first offender, however,

and got off more easily with imprisonment. The jury had
made an intelligent legal distinction without statutory
guidance, and this fact undeniably supported their invest-
ment with discretionary powers, at least in this particular
case. James Crampton was no less an unsympathetic character;
he had shot his wife while she was on the toilet. Neither
case augured well for the LDF.[47]

Before either appeal was decided, several promising
developments occured for the abolitionists. A Fourth
Circuit U.S. Court of Appeals Suit, Ralph v. Warden,[48]
ruled that the death penalty, where a rapist did not take
or endanger the life of his victim, was cruel and unusual
punishment. The decision had its problems though. It did
not rule the death penalty unconstitutional in all rape
cases, and therefore acknowledged by implication that in
at least some instances, a death sentence for rape might be
appropriate. The dissent in the case scored this distinction: "The permissible punishment in a rape case may depend
entirely upon whether the victim submitted or resisted."[49]
Nevertheless, the Circuit Court, by its three to two ruling
had indicated that at least some judges were interested
in maintaining the viability of the Eighth Amendment as an
approach to dealing with capital punishment.

Then in December 1970, the lame duck Governor of

Arkansas, Winthrop Rockefeller, commuted all fifteen death
sentences in the state to life, commenting that "what
earthly mortal has the omnipotence to say who among us shall
live and who shall die? I do not."[50]   He then urged all
other governors to follow his example. Less than a month
later, outgoing Attorney General of Pennsylvania, Fred
Speaker, decided to act on his convictions too. He ordered
the state's electric chair removed, and the chamber housing
it turned into an office. The Death Row inmates were put
into the general prison population. Speaker's authority
to act thusly was challenged, but none of the new officials,
including Governor Milton Shapp, moved to reverse the actions.
The chair was not replaced.[51]   The Fund's protracted court
battle against capital punishment was perhaps also having
a salutary effect on government officials.

    The decision in McGautha and Crampton was handed down
on May 3, 1971, and although its contents did not come as
a total surprise to the Fund lawyers, the six to three
ruling against the discretion and single verdict issues was
nonetheless disheartening. Justice Harlan wrote for the
majority that the states were entitled to assume that jurors,
faced with a life or death decision, would act responsibly.
Standards, furthermore, simply were not feasible: "To
identify before the fact those characteristics of criminal

homicides and their perpetrators which call for the death
penalty, and to express these characteristics in language
which can be fairly understood and applied by the sentencin
authority, appear to be tasks which are beyond present
human ability."[52] On the single verdict question, the
Court recognized the tension between constitutional rights
which existed, but concluded that the scope of the Fifth
Amendment was not so broad as to free a defendant from all
"adverse consequences" if he took the witness stand.[53]

The dissents of Justices Douglas, Marshall, and
Brennan blasted the majority's reasoning. The first point
of contention was that the Court was ruling against a precedent which was relevant to the present situation. In a
1966 case, Giaccio v. Pennsylvania,[54] the Court had overturned a statute which permitted a jury to fix the courtroom costs for an acquitted defendant as it saw fit. Justi
Black at the time had written: "It is established that a
law fails to meet the requirements of the Due Process Claus
if it is so vague and standardless that it...leaves judges
and jurors free to decide, without any legally fixed standards, what is prohibited and what is not in each particular
case."[55] Yet the majority text, save for a single footnote
had ignored the implications of Giaccio.

Justice Brennan particularly scored the majority

.

view that standards of some sort could not be worked out.
He noted that such reasoning

> ...reaches conclusions substantially identical
> with the following urged in 1785 by Archdeacon
> William Paley to justify England's 'Bloody Code'
> of more than 250 capital crimes: 'The selection
> of proper objects for capital punishment depends
> upon circumstances, which, however easy to perceive
> in each particular case after the crime is committed,
> it is impossible to enumerate or define beforehand;
> or to ascertain, however, with that exactness, which
> is requisite in legal descriptions.' 56

Brennan then hammered home his point. Even if perfect
standards are impossible, he continued, that alone should
not "justify making no attempt whatsoever to control law-
less action."[57] States had a fundamental obligation to
clarify their policies with regard to capital sentencing.
The procedural regularity required by the Due Process
Clause in capital cases, Brennan argued, demanded that defendants be sentenced on some consistent notion of penological
policy.[58] The system of investing juries with full discretionary powers was at odds with this goal.

To the Fund lawyers, McGautha must have seemed like
the end of the road. An Eighth Amendment challenge to
capital punishment still lay ahead, but a favorable adjudication in such a case now seemed all the less likely.
Justice Black, regardless of the fact that the issue had
not even been raised for argument, had gratuitously inserted

into his <u>McGautha</u> concurring opinion that the Eighth
Amendment was no impediment to capital punishment's constitutionality.[59] Besides the hostility inherent in this
act, Fund lawyers realized that the Court had rejected an
opportunity to overturn nearly all capital sentences in
the United States without necessarily having to eliminate
the death penalty as a punishment option in all cases.
Certainly if the Justices were interested in restricting
capital punishment, the standards and single verdict issues
provided them with a chance to do so in a manner which woul
probably minimize public protest. To rule the death penalty unconstitutional as cruel and unusual punishment
would require a daring and outlook the present Court did
not appear to have.

Less than two months after the <u>McGautha</u> verdict, the
Court announced that it would review four cases (<u>Furman</u> v.
<u>Georgia</u>, <u>Aikens</u> v. <u>California</u>, <u>Jackson</u> v. <u>Georgia</u>, and
<u>Branch</u> v. <u>Texas</u>) in order to determine if the death pen-
alty constituted cruel and unusual punishment.[60] Two of
the death sentences involved were for murder (<u>Furman</u> and
<u>Aikens</u>) and the other two were for rape (<u>Jackson</u> and <u>Branch</u>
All four of the defendants were blacks whose victims had
been white. Before the oral argument was held, however,
both Justice Black and Justice Harlan resigned from the

Court for health reasons. The delay in confirming their
successors, Lewis F. Powell, Jr. and William H. Rehnquist,
permitted two encouraging anti-capital punishment developments to occur in other courts.

On January 17, 1972, the New Jersey Supreme Court
struck down the state's death penalty statute on the basis
of the 1968 U.S. v. Jackson decision.[61] Originally, in 1968,
the New Jersey Supreme Court had determined that the state's
capital punishment provision did not come under the Jackson
ruling, but on appeal, the U.S. Supreme Court had simply
reversed and remanded the case, without hearing arguments.[62]
Consequently, the New Jersey Supreme Court felt bound to
invalidate the capital punishment law in New Jersey, though
Chief Justice Weintraub indicated that personally, he was
not pleased: "I regret to say that the Federal Supreme
Court's handling of this important subject is not my idea
of effective judicial administration. An appeal to the
highest authority...should be more rewarding than a trip to
Delphi."[63] Nevertheless, the Fund was not going to argue
with the result, which was no more capital punishment in
New Jersey.

The more significant action was taken by the California
Supreme Court, which on February 18, 1972 announced that
capital punishment was unconstitutional under the state

constitution's "cruel _or_ unusual" punishment clause.[64]
The decision eliminated the country's largest Death Row
population, and since it was based on the state constitution,
it was unreviewable by the U.S. Supreme Court.[65] Although
Governor Reagan angrily denounced the ruling as a "case of
the courts setting themselves up above the people and the
legislature," and threatened to appeal, it was clear that
only a constitutional amendment could change the result.[66]
The reasoning of the court's six to one majority was firmly
based on the _Trop_ concept of "evolving standards of decency,'
and contended that an informed public would reject the
death penalty's use. Amsterdam had argued this point un-
successfully before the Federal Supreme Court in _Boykin_,
but now, three years later in California, a major court had
subscribed to his logic. Namely, people only accepted capital punishment in theory, not in practice. It was solely
the rare and discriminatory imposition of death which allowed the citizenry to support capital punishment. As
Amsterdam would reason in his _Furman_ brief, "if the penalty
of the law were generally, even-handedly, non-arbitrarily
enforced in all of the cases to which it applied...the
public conscience of the Nation would be profoundly and
fundamentally revolted."[67] The California Supreme Court
agreed. Furthermore, the court was not buying the argument

that this sort of determination was solely a legislative one.
"The cruel or unusual punishment clause" of the state constitution, the Justices wrote, "operates to restrain legislative and executive action and to protect fundamental
individual and minority rights against encroachment by the
majority."[68] Here was a no-holds barred adjudication.

The Federal Supreme Court could not fail to be influenced by such a decision. The California Supreme Court
was known for its legal trailblazing and sound scholarship.
Its decisions inevitably had a strong impact on the legal
world. As Amsterdam said, "the California Supreme Court
is to the courts what U.C.L.A. is to basketball."[69] The
capital punishment ruling was all the more persuasive coming from a state where public opinion heavily favored the
death penalty, and where the Death Row population was over
a hundred, and included such notorious figures as Sirhan
Sirhan and Charles Manson.[70] Acting in the face of a
country increasingly inclined to social conservatism, the
California Supreme Court had set an example which was not
easily ignored.

The LDF brief in Furman tried to outline logically an
approach for the U.S. Supreme Court to take in weighing
the validity of capital punishment apropos to the Eighth
Amendment. First, the Eighth Amendment was a dynamic and

evolving standard; it was not static. What was permissible
in the eighteenth century might be condemned in the twentieth.
Second, the Court would not be infringing upon a legislative perogative if it held that capital punishment was
"cruel and unusual." The inclusion of the Eighth Amendment
into the Bill of Rights necessarily meant that courts would
have to render judgments on legislatively approved punishments. Third, the infrequent and rare use of the death
penalty was apposite in determining that capital punishment
was "cruel and unusual." Fourth, the Court should look
to "enlightened" conceptions of "decency" and "human dignity." Specifically, Amsterdam argued:

> The question is not: will contemporary stand-
> ards of decency allow the existence of such a gen-
> eral law on the books? The question is, rather:
> will contemporary standards of decency allow the
> general application of the law's penalty in fact?
> The distinction which we draw here lies between
> what public conscience will allow the law to say
> and what it will allow the law to do.71

Fifth, capital punishment was disproportionately severe for
rape. Sixth, a punishment is "unnecessarily" harsh and
violates the Constitution if a lesser penalty serves the
same purpose. And finally, the physical and the psychological sufferings of the inmates on Death Row were Eighth
Amendment considerations.72

When the Furman decision was handed down on June 29,

1972. The Fund's arguments had won out by the slimmest of margins. In what can only be described as a verbose 243 pages consisting of nine separate opinions, the Court ruled five to four that capital punishment was unconstitutional under the Eighth Amendment as applied to the states by the Fourteenth Amendment.[73] The actual results of the five separate opinions in the _Furman_ decision were the following: all of the 631 men and 2 women on death rows in 32 states were entitled to new sentences of life imprisonment, or perhaps less; the capital punishment statutes in the 39 states which still provided for the death penalty were invalidated.[74] Except for these conclusions, however, which the five justices agreed on, the meaning of _Furman_ was not certain. Three Justices (Douglas, Stewart, and White) argued that capital punishment was "cruel and unusual" in the mode of its imposition. Douglas contended that the death penalty was discriminatory:

> A law that stated that anyone making more than $50,000 would be exempt from the death penalty would plainly fall, as would a law that in terms said that blacks, those who never went beyond the fifth grade in school, those who made less than $3,000 a year, or those who were unpopular or unstable should be the only people executed. A law which in the overall view reaches that result in practice has no more sanctity than a law which in terms provides the same.[75]

White and Stewart only saw the administration of the death

penalty as arbitrary. Stewart explained:

> These death sentences are cruel and unusual in the same way that being struck by lightning is cruel and unusual...The Eighth and Fourteenth Amendments cannot tolerate the infliction of a sentence of death under legal systems that permit this unique penalty to be so wantonly and so freakishly imposed.[76]

The opinions of these three justices, taken together, formed the largest common denominator of the decision. Their area of agreement represented the rule of the case which future judges would consider binding precedent.

Chief Justice Burger tried to sum up _Furman_'s practical effect: "If the legislatures are to continue to authorize capital punishment for some crimes, juries and judges can no longer be permitted to make the sentencing determination in the same manner they have in the past."[77] Conceivably then, an opening had been left for the return of capital punishment. Douglas, Stewart and White had found the meaning of the Eighth Amendment in terms of other constitutional standards. The actual facts and effects of the death penalty's application, not the punishment per se, rendered capital punishment "cruel and unusual." If the defects in administration were satisfactorily remedied, by mandatory laws for example, the states could revive the death penalty in a constitutional

form. This approach, however, virtually robbed the
Eighth Amendment of any independent effect on capital
punishment.[78] In essence, this trio of Justices was saying that it was the violation of Due Process requirements
which established capital punishment as "cruel and unusual."

The other two judges in the majority, Thurgood Marshall and William Brennan, left no room for a remedial
approach to capital punishment. The death penalty was
cruel and unusual because it was inconsistent with present
day morals and values, as evidenced by the decreased
number of executions, the search for more human methods of
killing, and the refusal to hold public executions.
Brennan argued that "when an unusually severe punishment is
authorized for wide-scale application but not, because
of society's refusal, inflicted save in a few instances,
the inference is compelling that there is a deep-seated
reluctance to inflict it. Indeed," he continued, "the
likelihood is great that the punishment is tolerated only
because of its disuse."[79] In this sense, public opinion
polls were misleading, because they did not measure society's acceptance of an even-handed and prevalent application of the death penalty.

Justice Marshall went one step further. He theorized
that public support for capital punishment was largely

based on ignorance, and that rational persuasion and
wider dissemination of knowledge as to the utilitarian
and humanitarian aspects of the death penalty would evoke
a change in public sentiment. "Assuming knowledge of all
the facts presently available regarding capital punishment,
the average citizen would, in my opinion, find it shocking
to his conscience and sense of justice."[80] Marshall's
theory, if true,[81] would also undercut the argument that
since forty-one states had death penalty laws, that fact
was the true measure of the people's will. The public's
lack of exposure to the death penalty, Marshall argued,
leads to indifference, which in turn, inevitably preserves
the status quo. To the extent that retribution was the
foundation for the nation's support of the death penalty,
Marshall held that vengeance as a sole basis for a statute
was an impermissible societal goal.

Taken together, Brennan and Marshall's judicial approach was essentially a normative one, which defined
standards underlying the Eighth Amendment, and tried to
apply to them current public mores and opinions. This
analysis required an external orientation to societal values
based on the available objective evidence.[82] Chief Justice
Burger argued that "data of more recent vintage are essential" if one is to gauge the actual and constitutionally

relevant viewpoints of the public on the death penalty.[83]
Marshall countered that the indications were strong enough
to lend weight to the conclusion that the people would not
knowingly tolerate the reality of capital punishment.

The four Nixon appointees, Burger, Blackmun, Powell,
and Rehnquist each filed dissents stressing that the Court
was overstepping its sphere of authority and usurping legislative powers. Blackmun wrote:

> Were I a legislator, I would vote against the
> death penalty for the policy reasons argued by counsel
> for the respective petitioners... [this] authority
> should not be taken over by the judiciary in the
> modern guise of an Eighth Amendment issue....It is
> impossible for me to believe that the many lawyer-
> members of the House and Senate...were callously un-
> aware and insensitive of constitutional overtones
> in legislation of this type.[84]

Powell sounded a similar argument: "Legislative judgments
as to the efficiency of particular punishments are pre-
sumptively rational and may not be struck down under the
Eighth Amendment because this Court may think that some
alternative sanction would be more appropriate."[85]

Chief Justice Burger emphasized a slightly different
point. He saw the majority opinion as a Due Process argument couched in Eighth Amendment terms: "It would be dis-
ingenuous to suggest that today's ruling has done anything
less than overrule McGautha in the guise of an Eighth

Amendment adjudication."[86] According to Burger, the
McGautha decision under the principle of stare decisis
should have been controlling.

The majority opinions firmly defended the validity
of the Court's taking action. Brennan explained that the
Justices "must not, in the guise of 'judicial restraint'
abdicate [their] fundamental responsibility to enforce
the Bill of Rights."[87] The Eighth Amendment specifically
was a limit on the punishments a legislature could codify
into law, and therefore the Court was required to make what
were, in essence, "legislative determinations" (e.g the
state of public opinion) in reviewing the constitutionality
of capital punishment. To do as the dissenters urged would
render the Eighth Amendment useless as a judicial instrument. The whole purpose of the "cruel and unusual" clause
was so that assembly mandated punishments would face re-
strictions. The existence of the Eighth Amendment in the
Bill of Rights indicated that the framers of the Constitution
did not intend to have legislatures police themselves on
this matter.

The Furman decision was the culmination of an almost
decade long legal struggle, spearheaded by the LDF, to
eliminate the death penalty in America. Abolitionist

reaction expressed general euphoria and unrestrained
enthusiasm and optimism. Jack Greenberg asserted straight
out that "there will no longer be any more capital punishment in the United States," and most death penalty opponents
agreed.[88] The possibility of the Court accepting state
legislative standards to guide the administration of
capital punishment seemed precluded as long as McGautha
remained as viable law. The majority there had explicitly
stated that standards were impossible to formulate properly,
and in any case, would not serve to limit jury discretion
substantially. Chief Justice Burger's dissent in Furman
confirmed this view: "There is little reason to believe
that sentencing standards in any form will substantially
alter the discretionary character of the prevailing system
of sentencing in capital cases."[89] The LDF felt confident
that the Court would not permit states to experiment with
standards to test their effect since human lives would be
at stake.

Nor was the Fund particularly concerned with states
trying to enact mandatory capital punishment statutes.
Even the Justices who wrote dissents seemed to agree that
mandatory death penalty laws were subject to serious flaws.[90]
History had already shown that to establish a jury "guilty"
verdict as synonymous to the order for an execution was to

run the high risk of upsetting the balanced administration of justice by tempting judges and juries to strain the law and the evidence whenever their sentiments so dictated.

If the LDF believed that constitutionally the death penalty was no longer workable, it also hoped that as a matter of public and legislative taste, capital punishment ultimately would be rejected. The continued absence of executions, in conjunction with a healthy political and economic climate, would most likely display abolition as a desirable objective for a nation. Yet capital punishment was not so easily eliminated from the country's system. The United States' emotional need for the death penalty rapidly made itself felt after the Furman decision. As is so often the case, an unused and impractical item becomes highly desirable when forcibly taken away. Although the comparison of capital punishment to a mothballed army uniform may not stand close inspection, the Fund lawyers were about to find out that one's useless but prized possessions are rarely relinquished with grace.

CHAPTER FIVE

    The signals from this Court have not...always
  been easy to decipher.
                    Chief Justice Warren Burger

    The nation wasted no time in putting the _Furman_
decision to the test. Because the majority opinions save
for Brennan's and Marshall's did not unequivocally state
that capital punishment in all forms was unconstitutional,
it was inevitable that the states would pass new death
penalty legislation which would try to meet the perceived
requirements of the _Furman_ ruling. As the New York Committee
to Abolish Capital Punishment commented: "The way has
been left open for state legislatures to attempt to re-
enact the death penalty in conformance with criteria
suggested by the Court's decision....While this will not
be an easy thing to do...it is unfortunately the kind of
thing that will appeal to certain legislators."[1]

    The problem though, was one of interpretation. What
did the verdict mean? Most abolitionists were confident
that no rewording of statutes could satisfy the objections
the Court had as to the application of the death penalty.
Others, however, felt that legislation which provided for
guided jury discretion by specifying aggravating and/or
mitigating circumstances for crimes might pass muster under

the _Furman_ standards. Still others felt that strictly
mandatory capital punishment laws were the only option
left available by the _Furman_ decision.

This state of general confusion was reflected in the
variety of new legislation that was enacted. North Carolina,
for example, instituted a mandatory death penalty by judicial fiat. The State Supreme Court simply interpreted
Furman as invalidating the discretionary aspects of the
old law. In Louisiana and perhaps fourteen other states,
the legislatures enacted mandatory capital punishment
statutes for a specified list of crimes.[2] Florida, Texas,
Georgia and as many as seventeen other states passed capital punishment legislation which designated criteria to
serve as guidelines for the discretionary imposition of
the death penalty. California reacted to the _Anderson_ and
Furman decisions by passing a constitutional amendment. In
New Jersey, Governor Brendan Byrne indicated that he would
hold off signing new capital punishment legislation until
a clarifying decision was handed down from the Supreme
Court indicating exactly what would be constitutional.
Massachusetts and South Dakota enacted new laws which were
then vetoed by their Governors. Kansas and North Dakota
took no action at all towards restoring the death penalty.[3]

The speed with which all this legislation was passed

was a testimonial to the nation's fervent desire to have
capital punishment laws on the books. Even the cost of living index seemed to grow slower than the number of capital
punishment laws and Death Row inmates across the country.
Proposition 17, reinstituting the death penalty, was over-
whelmingly voted in by California voters barely four months
after Furman. In Florida, Governor Reubin Askew signed the
death penalty back into law on December 8, 1972. By mid-
1973, thirteen states had restored capital punishment,
while sixteen had death penalty bills pending in their legislatures. By the end of 1973, twenty-three states were
back in the business of sentencing criminals to death, and
a total of forty-four prisoners were on Death Row. On
March 13, 1974, the U.S. Senate, by a 54 to 33 vote placed
the Federal Government into the swelling number of capital
punishment jurisdictions. One more year saw a total of 31
states with capital punishment laws, and a total of 207
condemned prisoners. As the nation's bicentennial approached, 34 states had restored capital punishment, and fully 611
persons were awaiting their deaths.[4] Yet these condemned
inmates were in legal abeyance. They could not be executed,
for no one knew if any, all or none of the new statutes
were constitutionally permissible by Furman standards. The
only certainty was that the Supreme Court would have to

issue a clarifying ruling.

The Court's Turnaround

The edict of the Court was handed down on July 2, 1976, two days shy of the country's two-hundredth birthday, and no doubt many abolitionists were thinking of the irony if the decision restored an archaic mode of punishment during the nation's celebration of the past. Although five verdicts in capital punishment related appeals were announced, the crucial opinion was contained in the case of Gregg v. Georgia.[5] A seven to two majority of the Court stated flat-out: "We now hold that the punishment of death does not invariably violate the Constitution."[6] The fireworks were starting early.

The majority opinion, written by Justice Stewart, announced the criteria for interpreting the Eighth Amendment: 1. the punishment must involve no unnecessary or wanton pain; 2. "the punishment must not be grossly out of proportion to the severity of the crime."[7] The key point, however, was the Court's presumption of the validity of legislatively enacted punishment:

> We may not require the legislature to select
> the least severe penalty so long as the penalty
> selected is not cruelly inhumane or disproportionate
> to the crime involved. And a heavy burden rests
> on those who would attack the judgment of the rep-
> resentatives of the people.[8]

The fact that thirty-four states and the Federal Government had re-enacted the death penalty, the Court contended, undercut the petitioners' claims that "evolving standards of decency" could no longer tolerate capital punishment.

The majority view was a straight rejection of the LDF's arguments. The Court completely failed to review the nature of public support for the death penalty. Legislatures, the Fund had argued time and again, were a misleading reflection of the public will. Rather, the constitutionally relevant questions were three: 1. would public opinion in support of capital punishment remain steadfast in the face of an evenhanded, widespread use of the death penalty?; 2. was public opinion in support of capital punishment founded on misinformation, which if corrected, would erode that support?; 3. was public opinion in support of capital punishment based on a legislatively and judicially unacceptable goal, such as retribution or discrimination? The Court, however, believed that these determinations were best left to the legislatures, and refused to give weight to the recent empirical evidence which tended to support the LDF's arguments.[9]

In essence, the Court's approach was an abdication of its responsibility to enforce the Bill of Rights. The concept underlying the Eighth and many of the other

Amendments is nothing less than the protection of minority rights against the tyranny of the majority. To permit the legislature, the embodiment of the people's will, to have sole responsibility for determining the legitimacy of a punishment applied infrequently to an unpopular few, essentially means that that very same legitimacy will go unchallenged. If the people and their representatives were normally ceded the last word on constitutional issues, no doubt freedom of speech or abortion rights, to name two examples, would be severely curtailed. The Supreme Court has a fundamental obligation to make its own independent determination on these matters, and to rule accordingly.

The Court's logic in _Gregg_ basically stripped the Eighth Amendment of any real authority. The sole role of the Amendment was now limited to overturning a situation where, for instance, one or two states instituted branding or mutilation or some other such barbarity. Yet if thirty-five states adopted similar legislation, that fact in itself presumably would be the measure of the punishment's constitutional acceptability. The _Gregg_ verdict dictated that a penalty must be proportionate to the crime involved, but then inexplicably tied the determination of that proportionality to a dubious measure of public support for the particular punishment.

The majority opinion also attempted to defend the role of retribution as "an expression of society's moral outrage at particularly offensive conduct....This function," the Court explained "...is essential in an ordered society that asks its citizens to rely on legal processes rather than self-help to vindicate their wrongs."[10] Yet was anyone seriously contending that vigilanteism or lynching would result from the abolition of the death penalty? The Court failed to consider adequately whether the death penalty was essential to the satisfactory fulfillment of retributive urges. If, as is the implication, life imprisonment cannot perform this function, then it is hard to understand why the Court extends consitutional toleration to imprisonment as a penalty for some murders. If on the other hand, life sentences can satisfy vengeance desires, then the death penalty serves no legitimate legislative purpose.[11]

The greatest problem for the Court, however, was to reconcile the Gregg decision with precedent. Furman by itself presented little problem in this area: "The concerns in Furman that the penalty of death not be imposed in an arbitrary or capricious manner can be met by a carefully drafted statute that ensures that the sentencing authority is given adequate information and guidance."[12] More specifically, the Court explained, Furman held only that a death

penalty decision "had to be guided by standards so that
the sentencing authority would focus on the particularized
circumstances of the crime and the defendant."[13] The com-
plications arose when McGautha was introduced. Quite simply,
the McGautha contention that the drafting of sentencing
guidelines and standards was unworkable (see p. 127) and
"beyond present human ability," was a direct contradiction
of the holding in Gregg. If Furman is interpreted in light
of the McGautha ruling, as it must be, it is clear that
guided discretionary sentencing was not meant to be a
constitutionally viable alternative. The only option that
Furman in conjunction with McGautha did not specifically
eliminate, as Justice Douglas noted in his opinion at the
time, was the mandatory imposition of the death penalty.[14]

The majority opinions discounted the claim that
arbitrariness would still exist under the Georgia statute
due to prosecutorial judgments and more subtle forms of
jury discretion. Justice White wrote: "Petitioner's argument...seems to be in final analysis an indictment of our entire
system of justice....I decline to interfere with the manner
in which Georgia has chosen to enforce such laws on what is
simply an assertion of lack of faith in the ability of the
system of justice to operate in a fundamentally fair manner."[15] The Court particularly stressed that the statute's

provision for automatic appeals to the Georgia Supreme
Court would have a balancing-out influence, and would
tend to standardize the imposition of the death penalty.

The fundamental assumption behind the Court's reasoning was that death is not a unique enough penalty of the
law to justify anything more than standards which theoretically provide the opportunity to have death imposed in a
"fair" manner. The Fund, as Amsterdam had contended in
oral argument, was saying "no, our argument is essentially
that death is different. If you don't accept the position
that death is different, we lose the case."[16] The Fund
was trying to convince the Court that equal end results
from the new statutes were still highly unlikely, and that
regardless of any possibility to the contrary, the gravity
of the issue should disallow what basically amounted to
experimentation with human lives.

Along with Gregg, two other decisions announced the
same day upheld guided discretionary capital punishment
statutes in Florida and in Texas.[17] The common ground of
the three rulings seemed to establish the following conditions for constitutional death penalty legislation: 1.
a bifurcated trial in which the second stage was devoted
entirely to sentencing; 2. statutory description of both
aggravating and mitigating circumstances to control the

sentencing; 3. state appellate review of the legal and
factual basis for the sentencing decision that was
reached.[18] In the final two rulings of July 2, 1976, however, the Court struck down by a five to four vote mandatory death penalties in North Carolina and Louisiana.[19]
The abolitionists had not completely lost the day. These
latter two decisions would involve resentencing to imprisonment approximately 170 Death Row inmates in the two states,
and perhaps eventually as many as 300 across the country.[20]

The Court had reasoned that the historical antipathy
to mandatory death penalties was relevant in interpreting
"contemporary standards of decency." Justice Stewart's
majority opinion explained: "We believe that in capital
cases the fundamental respect for humanity underlying the
Eighth Amendment requires consideration of the character
and record of the individual offender and the circumstances
of the particular case."[21] The logic behind this belief,
however, sounded suspiciously like the LDF's brief in Gregg,
for the Court went on to comment that "the penalty of death
is qualitatively different from a sentence of imprisonment,
however long."[22] In this light, the Gregg opinion becomes
even harder to justify. The Justices had recognized the
unique nature of death as a sanction, yet it was only in
conjunction with either mandatory or unlimited discretion

death penalty statutes that this perception aroused the
Court's disapproval of capital punishment. The Court
failed to explain the distinguishing characteristic of
guided discretion statutes that exempted them from in-
validation under the "death is different" principle.

In a sense, the Court's five decisions were the
ultimate proof of the abolitionist contention that the
death penalty can never be applied even handedly and equitably. Gregg, a hitchhiker who robbed and slew the two men
who gave him a ride, had his death sentence affirmed. The
defendant in the North Carolina case (Woodson), who robbed
and killed a storekeeper, had his death sentence overturned.
Could the Court, or anyone for that matter, honestly contend that there was a basis for distinguishing between
these two criminals? Quite simply, if Gregg had committed
his crime in North Carolina and Woodson his crime in Georgia,
the post-litigative positions of the two men would have
been reversed.

"Let's Do It!"

For the men who remained on Death Row after the July
Second decisions, execution was not an immediate threat.
The Gregg verdict, by prescribing close inspection of
mitigating circumstances, opened up new channels of appeal

that promised to be long and tedious. Aryeh Neier of the
ACLU explained that "the major thing we're going to try to
do is block executions. If that means going to Court, to
the legislatures, or making a lot of fuss, we'll do that."[23]
Even if judicial abolition of capital punishment no longer
seemed a likely possibility, many techniques remained a-
vailable to abolitionist forces for forestalling executions.
Each condemned prisoner's case could be appealed. Governors could be petitioned for grants of clemency. Legislative
lobbying could focus on stopping the enactment of new death
penalty statutes and on repealing old ones. Public demonstrations could put pressure on public officials to take
action. Because Gregg mandated that a full opportunity
be given to the defendant to present favorable mitigating
evidence, extra legal help at the sentencing stage of a
trial might considerably reduce the imposition of death
sentences in the first place.[24] The net effect of all
these approaches abolitionists hoped, would be to prevent
the carrying out of any executions for at least two to
three years. If executions became unavoidable after that
period, then they still hoped to limit them as much as
possible.

    This strategy seemed to be developing without any
hitches until a Utah jury sentenced thirty-five-year-old

Gary Gilmore to death. Gilmore created a problem for
anti-capital punishment forces by trying to waive his
right to appeal: "I believe I was given a fair trial,
and I think the sentence was proper, and I'm willing to
accept it like a man and wish it to be carried out without
delay."[25] This type of reaction was not unusual for condemned men, but it presented abolitionists with a dilemma.
To permit a prisoner's demand for his death sentence to
be carried out was to concede that the state had a right
to execute. Abolitionists generally were willing to make
no such concession.[26] ACLU director Neier explained their
position: "Our quarrel is with the state, not with Gary
Mark Gilmore....To defer to the choice Mr. Gilmore has made
is to acknowledge the right of the state to engage in a
savagery and to coerce Mr. Gilmore into becoming an accomplice in a legal homicide."[27] The battle stage was set.

Gilmore did all he could to stave off any interventions
on his behalf, and in doing so, probably increased people's
commitment to saving him. He flatly told the ACLU to
"butt out," and tried to anger the LDF by writing to
them: "Look boy, I am a white man. Get that through
your brillo pad heads."[28] With people nevertheless trying
to forestall his execution, Gilmore found himself in the
position of having to dare the state into action: "Don't

the people of Utah have the courage of their convictions?
You sentenced a man to die - me - and when I accept the
extreme punishment with all grace and dignity, the people
of Utah want to back down and argue with me about it. You
are silly."[29] The bizarreness of the situation was emphasized all the more when Gilmore twice attempted suicide,
both times only to be saved by prison authorities rushing
him to the hospital. As one official pointed out, "by
what rationale is his suicide to be prevented by the very
society that demands his death?"[30]

The publicity attendant to the circumstances of Gilmore's situation was hardly surprising. Not only did Gilmore threaten to be the first person executed in the United
States in ten years, but he wanted to be! Yet the carnival-
like atmosphere and exploitation that did occur was more
than most people expected. The man who asked to be
executed was news, and the American public ate it up!
Gilmore received as many as two hundred letters a day, many
from women who wanted to marry him.[31] Warden Samuel Smith
needed five men for the firing squad, and got over two
dozen volunteers.[32] Gilmore's suicide pact with his lover,
Nicole Barrett, made front page headlines all over. All
these incidents and more, marked America's gory fascination
with death.

Agent Lawrence Schiller, with Gilmore's permission, took charge of marketing the macabre affair. Schiller, who had exclusive rights to the Jack Ruby shooting Lee Harvey Oswald photo and to many erotic Marilyn Monroe pictures, was a man with an eye for capitalizing on, as he put it, "unwarranted, uncalled-for deaths."[33] The success of Schiller's promotion of Gilmore was remarkable. Playboy paid twenty thousand dollars for a twenty-four thousand word interview, book rights were sold for half a million dollars, and ABC TV commissioned a six hour film for an unspecified, but no doubt lucrative, contract. Out of this payroll, Gilmore and his family were guaranteed sixty thousand dollars, Nicole Barrett and her mother twenty-five thousand dollars, and the families of Gilmore's victims forty thousand dollars. "There's no question that journalism feeds on deaths," explained Schiller, and the Gary Gilmore case was no exception.[34] Gilmore in essence became a media hero.

Gilmore's execution was set for January 17, 1977, and the intensity of this drama peaked the night before his scheduled death. Federal Judge Ritter had been prevailed upon to grant a last minute stay of execution at 1:05 a.m. Consequently, angered state officials had gotten the entire Tenth Circuit Court of Appeals out of bed at 4:15 a.m. to

hear arguments on setting aside the postponement. At
7:30 a.m., the stay was overruled. Thirty-seven minutes
later, after he had urged "let's do it!" Gilmore was dead
with four thirty caliber bullets through his heart.[35] The
moratorium was over.

Post-Gilmore Developments

The Gilmore execution did not open a floodgate of
new executions as some had feared. First of all, most
other Death Row inmates were not waiving their appeal rights
Perhaps as important an impediment to further executions,
though, was the circus-like flavor of the whole Gilmore
affair. As LDF director Greenberg commented: "We hope
that the circumstances of the Gilmore execution may in fact
hasten the demise of this racist, archaic, futile, and
barbarous institution."[36] The public and media reaction
throughout the whole ordeal did not reveal particularly
pleasant things about the nation's moral character. Many
advocates of capital punishment indicated that if future
executions had to be conducted in such a fashion, they
could no longer support capital punishment. In this sense,
the Gilmore execution was simultaneously a failure for the
abolitionists, in that a man died at the hands of the state,
and an embarrassment for the retentionists.

Gilmore's death may have had an enlightening effect on some state legislatures. As Deborah Leavy of the ACLU observed, "now that we're talking about real executions, perhaps [capital punishment] won't be so much of a political football."[37] In fact, Massachusetts, Kansas, New Mexico, and Hawaii each repulsed attempts to institute the death penalty after the Gilmore execution. Four months after the Utah spectacle, and almost a year after the Gregg and Woodson rulings, only twenty-seven states had the death penalty, and there were about 375 condemned prisoners.[38] Yet no one was overly enthusiastic. David Kendall of the LDF said: "I think the fact that there have not been a lot of executions yet by no means means there won't be."[39] Somebody's time, it seemed, was likely to run out soon.

Meanwhile, the Supreme Court was trying to clear up some of the loose ends in the Gregg verdict. Gregg had specifically dealt with the constitutionality of capital punishment as a sanction for murder. Now exactly one year later, in the case of Coker v. Georgia,[40] the Court ruled the death penalty unconstitutional for the rape of an adult. The basis for the decision was that "death is grossly disproportionate and excessive punishment for the crime of rape" as evinced by evolving standards of decency.[41] The Court used as its empirical foundation the fact that since

Furman, Georgia was the only state to reinstate capital
punishment for adult rapists, and that in ninety percent
of such cases, Georgian juries were not returning death
sentences.[42] In practical terms, the effect of _Coker_
was minimal, as only a few prisoners had to be resentenced.
However, the Court's holding that the death penalty "is an
excessive penalty for the rapist who, as such, does not
take human life,"[43] seemed to imply that the death penalty
for any crime which did not take human life, such as treason,
hijacking or kidnapping, would be unconstitutional. For
abolitionists, then, _Coker_ was an important victory which
limited the scope of capital crimes. The concomitant danger,
however, was that capital punishment as a whole might seem
more reasonable and just to the public since it was now
effectively limited to homicides as a penalty.

After the _Gregg_ decision abolitionists had been real-
istic in assessing the likelihood of a judicial abolition
of capital punishment. Greenberg had said: "The prospects
of a decision in the next few years effecting an across-the-
board abolition of the death penalty are now exceedingly
dim."[44] It was a slim possibility that newer and probably
weaker constitutional arguments would prevail where the
stronger and more familiar ones had failed.[45] Yet no one
was reconciled to giving up the fight. After _Gregg_ was

adjudicated, capital punishment opponents set out to do
what they had done once before in Furman: namely show
that the system was not working fairly or equitably.

A 1977 case, Gardner v. Florida,[46] indicated that
perhaps the rules set forth in Gregg, Jurek and Proffitt
were going to do little to limit arbitrariness in the
imposition of the death penalty. The defendant in the case
was convicted of first-degree murder, and after the sentencing hearing the jury returned with a recommendation
of life imprisonment. The trial judge, however, as he
was permitted to under Florida law, changed the sentence
to death, relying in part on a presentence court investi-
gatory report unavailable to the jury. The report was
neither disclosed to or requested by Gardner's counsel. On
appeal, the Florida Supreme Court did not review this
confidential information, nor consider the petitioner's
complaint against its use.

The Federal Supreme Court in a decision written by
Justice Stevens held that there was no basis for withholding
the report from the defendant's counsel, and that there
was even less foundation for not including the report as
part of the record for review by the state supreme court.
Justice Marshall, however, made an important argument in
his concurring opinion. The Court in Proffitt had assumed

that the Florida Supreme Court would be a standardizing factor in the imposition of death sentences, but it was clear in Gardner that the judges had simply rubber-stamped an approval of the death sentence. Marshall concluded, therefore, that the Supreme Court was obliged to reassess its holding in Proffitt. Not surprisingly, the Court took no such action, but Marshall had made a strong point.

In 1978, the Court was forced to refine still further the standards for administering the death penalty in the case of Lockett v. Ohio.[47] Lockett had driven the get-away car in the robbery/murder of a pawnbroker, and under Ohio law, she was as culpable as the triggerman. The Ohio capital punishment statute mandates death for a felony-murder offense unless: 1. the victim had induced or facil-itated the offense; 2. the defendant was under "duress, coercion, or strong provocation"; 3. the defendant's offense was the product of psychosis or mental deficiency.[48] Lockett met none of these conditions and was sentenced to death. The gunman, meanwhile, had plea bargained a prison sentence.

The Court faced a dilemma. Clearly the results in the present case were unacceptable, and yet the process by which they were reached seemed to satisfy the Gregg requirements. Chief Justice Burger started his opinion

with the understatement that "the signals from this
Court have not...always been easy to decipher."[49]   In
order to rationalize the verdict the Court was about to
hand down, Burger went on to conclude that "the States
now deserve the clearest guidance that the Court can provide; we have an obligation to reconcile previously dif-
fering views in order to provide that guidance."[50]   The
Ohio statute specified mitigating circumstances in accordance with the Gregg ruling, but the Court now held that
more was necessary: "To meet constitutional requirements,
a death penalty statute must not preclude consideration of
relevant mitigating factors."[51]   The Justices defined mitigating factors as: "Any aspect of a defendant's character or record and any of the circumstances of the offense
that the defendant proffers as a basis for a sentence less
than death."[52]   Specifically in Lockett's case, her mens
rea or "state of mind" was not investigated.   As Justice
Marshall wrote the felony-murder classification alone does
not "distinguish the intention or moral culpability of the
defendant."[53]

The practical effect of Lockett was to allow about
one hundred Ohio Death Row inmates to be resentenced.
Furthermore, an examination of the thirty-three states
which now had capital punishment indicated that perhaps

as few as nine would satisfy the new requirement of allow-
ing the presentation of enough mitigating factors.[54] Both
of these results created new opportunities for litigation
that would delay any upcoming executions. Yet the real
significance of Lockett lay in its ruling that "an individualized decision is essential in capital cases."[55] In
essence the Court was ceding strong discretionary power
back to the jury, at least in considering mitigating factors. This move seemed to promise that the same sort of
problem the Court had tried to eliminate in Furman would
reappear: arbitrariness.

Most recently, abolitionists have tried to compile
data that show the new statutes have not been working in a
constitutionally acceptable fashion. The case of John
Spenkelink,[56] a thirty-year-old Florida man sentenced to
die for murder, was chosen by Fund lawyers to present a new
challenge to capital punishment. The major line of attack
was the theory that the death penalty is imposed mainly in
cases where the victim is white. Sociologists William
Bowers and Glenn Pierce produced the following statistics
for the four year period from 1973-1977 in Florida:[57]

victim/offender race	number of offenders	persons sentenced to death	probability of death penalty
black kills white	286	48	.168
white kills white	2146	72	.034
black kills black	2320	11	.005
white kills black	111	0	.000

Yet neither the Florida appellate courts nor the Fifth
Circuit U.S. Court of Appeals found any merit in Spenkelink's
arguments. Finally, on March 26, 1979, the Supreme Court
announced its refusal to hear the case. The Court's reluctance to give a hearing to important empirical evidence
was very disheartening for abolitionists. Complained one
attorney, "the Court just doesn't want to hear about capital
punishment. They just threw the whole issue back to the
states and said, 'do what you will.'"[58] The immediate result is, as one defense lawyer summarized, that "there is
no longer any legal barrier to the execution of John
Spenkelink."[59]

Spenkelink and After

If the entire Gary Gilmore affair was treated at
times as an anomaly by both retentionists and abolitionists
alike, there was no denying the harsh reality of John
Spenkelink's execution in Florida's electric chair on May
25, 1979. Having spent seven years on death row, Spenkelink
and his attorneys, unlike Gilmore, had attempted and exhausted every avenue of legal appeal. Spenkelink evidenced
no suicide wishes, and indeed, fought the state every step
of the way in its attempt to put him to death. When the
voltage finally flowed that day, Spenkelink had the dubious

honor of being the first man in the United States to be
executed against his will since Aaron Mitchell in 1967.[60]

For abolitionists, the circumstances leading to
Spenkelink's execution epitomized the strongest argument
against the death penalty. No one was claiming that
Spenkelink was innocent, or clearly capable of rehabilitation -- merely that Spenkelink's crime was no different,
no worse, no better, than that of numerous other inmates
serving time among the regular prison population. LDF
Director Jack Greenberg emphasized the capricious nature
of the punishment as follows: "Spenkelink's crime was no
worse than tens of thousands for which lesser penalties
regularly are imposed. It was committed against a man who
sodomized and violently assaulted him. Spenkelink's
accomplice now freely walks the streets. The deliberate
murder of San Francisco's Mayor was this week sentenced to
five years."[61] The point, as it had been all along, was
that capital punishment inevitably was imposed on certain
inmates with an arbitrariness non-reconcilable with present day notions of due process and equal justice for all.
Which is not to say that Spenkelink did not have a fair
trial, or more than every reasonable chance for legal appeals.
Rather, it is that there still were no discernible standards
which justified why Spenkelink was dead while others like

him, who had committed similar crimes, were alive.[62]

In the years immediately following Spenkelink's
death, the United States witnessed three more executions,
but like Gilmore's each was "consensual" on the part of
the inmate. Having been quoted as saying "Commute me or
execute me. Don't drag it out,"[63] Jesse Walter Bishop was
put to death in Nevada's gas chamber on October 22, 1979.
Supreme Court Justices Marshall and Brennan in voting (in
the minority, seven to two) for a stay of Bishop's execution referred to the situation as a "state-administered
suicide."[64]

Almost a year-and-a-half later, on March 9, 1981,
Steven Timothy Judy was put to death in Indiana. Again,
like Gilmore and Bishop before him, Judy waived his last
chances for appeals. "I don't hold no grudges. This is my
doing. I'm sorry it happened."[65] Nonetheless, a fellow
death row inmate, Larry Williams, had attempted to intercede
on Judy's behalf, claiming that Judy's execution would have
an inhibiting effect on the Indiana Supreme Court's acceptance of William's pending challenge to that state's death
penalty statute. Again, the Supreme Court denied the stay
by a vote of seven to two.[66]

Finally, late at night on August 10, 1982, Frank J.
Coppola was executed in Virginia, after having stated that

it was his "sincere wish" to die.[67] Although Coppola dis-
missed his lawyers and dropped his appeals, others, such
as the ACLU and LDF, petitioned on his behalf for a stay
of execution on the grounds that it should await final
federal court approval of Virginia's capital punishment law,
to which a court challenge was pending. Obviously, if the
Virginia statute was overturned, slim as that possibility
might be, it would be inappropriate -- to say the least --
to have had someone executed under that same law. Again,
the stay was denied.[68]

Still, three executions over a span of nearly three
years can hardly be said to have reopened the floodgates of
capital punishment. For one, all three inmates actively
sought what for them was the perceived relief of execution.
Other death row prisoners were still obtaining stays of
execution while their various legal challenges wound their
way through lengthy appellate processes. And while few
persons were still looking to the Supreme Court to rule out
the constitutionality of capital punishment all together, a
couple of High Court adjudications did have corollary effects
in terms of granting new trials to certain death row inmates
and in further restricting the circumstances under which
death sentences could be imposed and/or carried out.[69]

Yet, at best, the Court's role could be said to be

supervisory, in that it had set down, primarily in Furman,
Gregg and Lockett, the courtroom guidelines under which
the death penalty might constitutionally be imposed, and
now was limiting itself to intervention only in such cases
where these standards were being bypassed or misimplemented.
Which was frequent enough to forestall numerous executions,
but not to the extent of eliminating them from the docket
altogether.

And additional pressure for a stepped-up pace of
executions was coming from the public-at-large, where the
death penalty was now a more attractive response to the
problem of crime than at any time over the last several
decades. A March 1981 Gallup Poll revealed that fully two-
thirds of all Americans favored the death penalty for those
persons convicted of murder.[70]

With this sort of public attitude, and with time
running out for numerous condemned inmates who have exhausted
their legal appeals, something clearly has to give. Benjamin
Rehnshaw, the acting director of the Bureau of Justice
Statistics has recently gone on record as predicting that
"The United States will witness a spate of executions
beginning in 1983-84 without parallel in this nation since
the Depression era."[71] With an approximate 1,150 inmates on
Death Row in a total of 37 states, he may be right.[72]

As this book goes to press, recent events indicate
that the issue of capital punishment in the United States
is about to come to a head. The first was the execution
in Texas on December 7, 1982 of Charles Brooks, Jr.[73] This
execution was significant in several of its aspects: 1) It
was the first ever administered by lethal injection;[74] 2) It
was the first execution of a black man since 1967; 3) Brooks,
like Spenkelink, had at no time waived any of his rights of
appeal; and 4) It again raised severe questions as to the
equitability with which the death penalty was imposed. In
separate trials, Brooks and an accomplice, Woody Lourdes, had
been convicted of murder. It was never determined which of
the two was the actual triggerman. Lourdes' original conviction, however, was overturned on a technicality involving
improper trial jury selection. Instead of going to a new
trial, Lourdes then pleaded guilty and received a sentence
of forty years (with the possibility of parole in six years).[7]

The irony of the situation was not lost on Jack
Strickland, who five years previously, had been the Terrant
County District Attorney handling Brooks' prosecution. Now
he found himself in the position of helping to file petitions
for a stay of Brooks' execution. As he succinctly explained,
"Is it appropriate for one man to get forty years and the
other death?"[76]

Perhaps the most significant aspect to Brooks'
execution was that it occured without a full hearing on
the merits of his last-minute appeal by the Fifth U.S.
Circuit Court of Appeals, even though the Federal District
Court in Texas had issued a "certificate of probable cause"
which typically calls for the Circuit Court to hold precisely such a review. The Fifth Circuit's actions were
then codified by the Supreme Court's six to three vote to
refuse a stay of execution for Brooks. As the three Justices
who dissented scathingly noted: "A Court of Appeals cannot
fulfill its obligation if a state is permitted to execute
a prisoner prior to the consideration and decision of his
appeal."[77]

Or as John Duncan, Texas Director of the ACLU put it,
"If you go to the Fifth Circuit, you will find a live appeal
and a dead plaintiff."[78] For all practical purposes, it
looked as though Brooks' death was the signal for executions
in the United States to begin proceeding at a quicker pace.
The message came through loud and clear: the failure to have
a full hearing and consideration of a last-minute appeal
was not in and of itself sufficient reason for granting a
stay of execution.

And yet, on January 25, 1983, barely six weeks later,
the Supreme Court issued a stay of execution for Thomas A.

Barefoot in a Texas capital case procedurally almost identical to that of Charles Brooks, Jr.[79] As in Brooks' case, the Fifth Circuit had rejected Barefoot's request for a stay of execution despite the fact that by filing a last-minute writ of habeas corpus, he had a formal appeal pending. This time, however, the Supreme Court stepped in and asked that attorneys on both sides prepare a full review of the procedure by which federal courts should handle all such last-minute appeals in capital punishment cases.[80]

Apparently the Court dissenters in the Brooks case had succeeded in convincing enough Justices this time around (too late to be of any benefit to Brooks it should be noted) that there was a valid legal quandary posed by the execution of a plaintiff with an appeal whose merits were still to be heard. From a practical viewpoint, the Court must also have been tempted to hear Barefoot's case by the realization that such situations would inevitably recur and continue to muddy the legal waters as well as consume a disproportionate amount of the Court's time. If instead, the Court could devise one set of minimum guidelines for handling last-minute appeals in capital cases, the standards could help eliminate the constant re-examination of appeals on a case-by-case basis. Only to the extent that a lower court failed to follow the set-out procedures might there then be grounds for a higher court review.

At present, oral arguments for the Barefoot case have been expedited, and are now set for April 26, 1983.[81] A decision is likely to arrive as soon as June or July of the same year. Until then, at least in the Fifth Circuit and in all likelihood elsewhere, it is relatively certain there will be no further executions. As Henry Schwarzchild, Director of the ACLU's Capital Punishment Project notes: "Obviously no court is going to deny us a stay while the Supreme Court decides under what conditions they may grant them."[82] But what then? It seems safe to assume that the Court's aim in Barefoot is not to impede further executions, but rather to set up lower court procedural guidelines for the review of last-minute appeals which will: 1) extricate the Court itself from the miasma of individual last-minute capital punishment appeals; and 2) facilitate the prompt implementation of states' capital punishment statutes without abrogating due process considerations.

Abolitionists would argue that establishing such a framework for the death penalty is impossible -- that the very nature of the United States' judicial system lends it-self to inconsistent results from case to case -- and that where death is the penalty, such a method of imposition is unacceptable. But every indication is that the majority of

the Supreme Court does not believe the foregoing to be
unworkable, and will use the Barefoot case to confront
the challenge of balancing due process considerations
insofar as last-minute appeals are concerned with the desire not to delay unreasonably the punishment process.
Indeed, the perceived policy benefits of capital punishment
are usually linked to its widespread and regular use as a
response to murder, and the Court may well decide that it
is finally time for the judiciary, by limiting its presence
at the forefront of the issue, to permit such a pattern of
imposition. If the adjudication of the Barefoot case
reflects such a philosophy, we can expect Benjamin Rehnshaw'
prediction of a "spate of executions" rapidly to become
reality.

The Outlook for the Future

The future of the death penalty in America appears
to rely on a curious dilemma. If the pace of executions
remains at one or two per year, there will be only a
minimal pressure to change or repeal capital punishment
statutes across the country. Without the reality and experience of frequent executions, people are more likely to
place a priority on the perceived policy benefits of having
capital punishment legislation on the books. On the other

hand, if all capital punishment laws are to be eliminated,
it may take the shock value of numerous executions to create
anything approaching a national revulsion towards the
death penalty. In this sense, the controversy of capital
punishment has shown itself to be of a perennial cyclical
nature. Both abolitionists and retentionists seem to
fight harder and win more victories when the opposing side
is holding the advantage. Like the incumbent politician,
the philosophy of punishment that prevails in any given
state is subject to attack on the job it has done. The
newcomer, who promises better results but has never been
forced to deliver, is then given a chance. Consequently
there are a surprising number of abolitions, restorations,
and re-abolitions of capital punishment. The long term
trend in America may well be towards a "higher civilization"
and the complete abolition of the death penalty, but it
is a progression marked by steady oscillation. For every
two steps forward the abolitionists take the nation, there
is at least one step backward directed by the retentionists.

The 1972 _Furman_ Supreme Court decision represented
the culmination of an abolitionist legal strategy. Since
then, however, the Court's activist nature has severely
diminished. Judicial restraint is the byword of the mid
and late Seventies, as well as the early Eighties, as the

Court has become particularly sensitive to charges of
judicial policy making after twenty years of strong intervention in social issues ranging from integration to
abortion. As Supreme Court analyst Robert McCloskey has
indicated: "The facts of the Court's history impellingly
suggest a flexible and non-dogmatic institution fully alive
to such realities as the drift of public opinion and the
distribution of power in the American republic."[83] At
present, the Court may well have done all one can expect
it to. Public opinion now strongly supports capital punishment, and the other branches of government have not given
the Court any encouragement to remain steadfast against
this trend.

It should be remembered that until 1963, no one really
gave a second thought to the idea of attacking capital
punishment through the judicial system. For close to two
hundred years all abolitionist activity had been directed
at the legislatures. No doubt Supreme Court involvement
in the capital punishment controversy affected legislators'
ideas of their duties and roles. The knowledge that the
Supreme Court was committed to evaluating capital punishment freed congressmen to acquiesce on the issue to their
constituencies. The lack of executions made the matter
seem all the more remote, and heightened the tendency of

lawmakers to succumb to local political pressures, misinformation, and ignorance. The response of Representative
Kastenmeier of Wisconsin to Professor Amsterdam's testimony
before a House Subcommittee in 1972 is one explanation of
the lack of responsibility legislators were wont to feel:

> Don't you feel that our colleagues in the
> Congress really have the basic question of whether,
> it being on the books, even if largely inoperative,
> these [capital punishment] laws do serve? Let us
> say they are unconvinced the removal will not re-
> move a form of deterrence and therefore, they are
> uncomfortable, particularly inasmuch as we seem to
> be having a crime wave in the country in the last
> few years, as to removing capital punishment, think-
> ing it does serve as a deterrent, without thinking
> through the matter quite as fully as you and others
> have. Isn't it sort of normal to expect them to
> come to that conclusion?[84]

The Congressman could have used a translator on that one.
The essence of the point he was making was nothing less than:
"Intuitively capital punishment is a deterrent, so how can
you expect Congressmen to risk political disfavor by actively
looking into this issue and fully considering the available
facts?" More recently, the Supreme Court's attempt to shift
responsibility back into the hands of the legislatures
seems to have been thwarted by similar "logic." The
fact that the Supreme Court has held capital punishment
to be <u>constitutional</u> seems to have implied to some lawmakers that capital punishment therefore automatically

becomes good <u>policy</u> and that no study of its pros and cons
is needed.

The deficiencies of American elected officials in
dealing with the capital punishment issue is emphasized
more fully when placed in a world context. Canada in
July 1976, after a period of experimental abolition, per-
manently outlawed the death penalty for all civilian crimes
by a 130-124 parliamentary vote.[85] About the same time,
Great Britain, which had abolished capital punishment many
years before, resisted attempts to reinstitute the death
penalty for terrorists convicted of murder. Despite polls
indicating that as much as 88% of the English public was
in favor of this bill. The House of Commons voted it down
361-232.[86] The conclusion is inescapable that England
and Canada's lawmakers, not having the option of abdic-
ating responsibility to an active federal judiciary, take
their obligations in a life and death issue more seriously
than their American counterparts.[87] It is unlikely that
any real shake-up in American legislative assumption of
responsibility will occur until the courts in this country
display a clear intention of limiting their intervention
in the capital punishment issue. Unfortunately, it seems
probable that only a resumption of regular executions will
make this point.

For the present, this breakdown of judicial and legislative willingness to oppose capital punishment will place a heavier burden on individual executives to use their clemency and pardoning powers. Of course, some dedicated abolitionists, like former governors Hugh Carey of New York and Jerry Brown of California, have previously and consistently acted on their beliefs and no doubt will continue to do so from whatever power bases they operate.[88] Mario Cuomo, the present Governor of New York, seems to come from the same mold. It is the marginally committed Governors, however, who may feel pressed into grants of clemency by the reality of impending executions. The recognition that only they stand between a man and his death if the courts fail to intercede can be expected to have a powerful effect on their actions. The tendency throughout history has been that whenever responsibility for a death decision can be isolated onto one person, executions are less likely to occur.[89]

If executives respond to the moral challenge of capital punishment by shifting towards abolitionist views, there will probably be an important secondary effect of influencing the public's position on capital punishment. People inevitably take cues from their leaders. It is hard to doubt that a speech like Richard Nixon's in 1973

calling for the restoration of the death penalty can be
a persuasive factor in the formation of some people's
opinions. Nixon had said: "Americans in the last decade,
were often told that the criminal was not responsible for
his crimes against society, but that society was responsible. I totally disagree with this permissive philosophy
....I am convinced that the death penalty can be an effective deterrent against specific crimes."[90] Yet at present,
few prominent national figures have risen to the challenge
of issuing a strong statement against capital punishment.[91]
Jimmy Carter, for all his talk of "human rights," failed
to see any contradiction between that policy and the maintenance of the death penalty in America. Ronald Reagan
considers abortion to be a crime against the sanctity of
human life, but conveniently fails to speak out against
the federal or state-run execution of condemned inmates.
The numerous executions in Iran in recent years have aroused
universal condemnation from American leaders, but no
accompanying re-examination of the United States' capital
punishment policy. If the American public is ever to rally
to the cause of abolition, stronger and less ambiguous
political leadership will have to be exerted.

Yet people are unlikely to diminish their support of
capital punishment unless they first recognize their own

retributive urges and attempt to channel them positively
by supporting rehabilitation as an additional goal of
punishment. As Gerald Gottlieb has written: "Corrective
institutions and systems must separate the dangerous mis-
creants from our midst, teach those who are teachable,
rehabilitate those who are rehabilitable, treat the mentally
ill who are treatable, and hold the others for treatments
as yet uninvented or undiscovered."[92] At present there
are critical impediments to the public's willingness to
subscribe wholeheartedly to this philosophy. A high crime
rate perceived as destroying the fabric of society lends
itself to the perpetuation of retributive justice. So too,
does a lack of willingness to trust parole boards to perform their functions properly. The impression that an
increasing number of criminals are "hard cases" or unre-
habilitable juveniles with no conception of morality also
leads a nation towards support of capital punishment.

Yet in the final analysis, advocacy of capital punishment inevitably reduces to revenge impulses of a dual nature.
The first is a sense of outrage at particularly atrocious
crimes. The other is the deep-rooted desire to extract
personal vengeance if a loved one is mercilessly slain.
Both are powerful emotional urges which will not necessarily
be dissuaded by rational argument.[93] Ultimately, these

feelings will only be brought under control through the development of a personal morality that places a higher value on the sanctity of human lives than on the horror in which one holds heinous crimes.

APPENDIX A

Taken from Gerald H. Gottlieb's <u>On</u> <u>Capital</u> <u>Punishment</u>, 7-9,
  ACLU Documents, XXXII.

        In <u>88</u> <u>Men</u> <u>and</u> <u>2</u> <u>Women</u> Warden Clinton T. Duffy describes
the first execution after he took over his job - that of
George Costello. Three days before his scheduled execution
Costello slashed his throat with a razor blade. This necessitated a postponement. Dr. W.P. Goddard wrote the warden
that "while Costello would probably be able to mount the
scaffold on schedule, the wound would open when he dropped,
considerable hemorrhaging would result, and the doctor
could not guarantee that the head wouldn't be completely
severed." The Governor granted a reprieve. Duffy reflects:
"This man had been granted a reprieve for the sole purpose
of giving him time to recover sufficiently for an execution
that would not be too messy."

        Some of Duffy's subjects marred the quietness of the
"perfect execution": the condemned do not always die grace-
fully. He describes a prisoner named Northcott at a period
before Duffy became warden and was Warden Holohan's secretary. Northcott claimed to have taken poison but, as it
proved, he was just "scared to death":

        "...'Must I see it all?' Northcott asked. 'Can't I
have a blindfold?' The warden, his face ashen, nodded, and
a black cloth was wrapped around the boy's eyes. His hands
shook so much that it took two guards to hold them in position long enough to be strapped together.

        "He was utterly petrified....

        "Behind me, I heard him sob, 'Please - don't make me
walk too fast.' I didn't have to turn around to know that
the guards were dragging him. He was almost limp when they
reached the foot of the gallows. As he was carried up the
thirteen steps, he let out a succession of hoarse cries
which increased in intensity until the big room sounded like
a madhouse."

        Former Row Chaplain, Byron E. Eshelman, wrote in <u>Death</u>
<u>Row</u> <u>Chaplain</u> of the execution of Robert Pierce, who was
about twenty-four at the time of his arrest for the murder
of a cab-driver. (The robbery had netted him about seven
dollars.) Pierce had spent three years on the Row and made

no secret of the fact that he planned to "die hard." The day before his "last elevator ride," Pierce kicked the toilet loose from his cell wall. He was placed in isolation.

The next morning, the chaplain approached Pierce's cell. The condemned man was covering his face with his hands, then looked up and grinned.

"Blood was pulsing from his neck," wrote Chaplain Eshelman.

A medical officer and a lieutenant of the guards hurried into the cell and Pierce tried to fight them off.

"They pinioned his arms, discovered a four-inch gash across the right side of his throat, all the way up to the ear."

The warden ordered four guards to drag Pierce from the holding cell and carry him into the gas chamber. He fought all the way down the corridor, screaming, "Lord... You know I'm innocent."

"'I'm innocent,' he screamed at the witnesses. 'Don't let me go like this. Oh, God!'

"Two witnesses got sick and had to leave."

Leandress Riley, too, had aroused concern that he would die "badly." When the final hour arrived, a guard unlocked his cell. Riley gripped the bars with both hands and began a long bone-chilling, wordless cry. The guards pulled him from the bars and stripped off his shirt and trousers. His flailing arms and legs were forced into a white shirt and blue denims.

The deep-throated cry continued, alternating with moaning and shrieking. Riley was carried to the gas chamber, fighting and writhing all the way. Using all their strength, the guards held him while the doctor taped the ends of the stethoscope in place.

The tension aroused in a condemned man awaiting the approach of the fatal hour is intolerable; often he chooses suicide as a solution to the anxiety and despair. A year after Pierce's execution, Eshelman writes, Oscar Brust, condemned for killing his wife and sixteen-year-old stepson, cut his throat with a piece of mirror the day before he was to go downstairs. Ralph Rogers, known as "little Navajo," jammed the lock of his cell with cloth, tied his mattress ticking to the ventilator grill, twisted the other end around his neck, and hung himself by stepping off the toilet seat. Boyd Van Winkle awaited his execution in the prison hospital. Each night he was given a sleeping pill. He "tongued" his pills until he had saved a lethal dose, then took them all one night. He never recovered from his coma.

Others, unable to stand the waiting, go insane. In The San Quentin Story, Warden Duffy discusses the case of Edwin Walker: "I shook Walker gently and spoke to him. He shrank from my touch and stared at me, but there was no recognition in his eyes. He seemed to be in a state of profound shock; his lips moved but made no sound.

"...The next morning, with the official witnesses waiting outside the gas chamber and the executioner standing by, seven consulting psychiatrists crowded into the little death cell to look at a broken shell of a man. Walker was mumbling to himself, crawling like a whipped dog on the floor, and hiding his head under a blanket. At intervals he burst into tears, and jumped wildly at the slightest touch. The doctors were unable to make him talk, and at 10 a.m., the hour set for Walker's death, they signed a statement declaring he had gone insane...."

For the condemned who can survive anxiety and despair while awaiting his hour without attempting suicide or going completely out of his mind, there is a final involuntary humiliation. Again and again, those about to be executed experience a loss of control of the sphincter muscles and find, to their horror, that they have soiled themselves. A natural relaxation of these muscles is a result of death; but for it to occur in advance of it can only be explained by the presence of uncontrollable and inordinate fear.

Dr. William F. Graves, during his period of service as a medical officer at San Quentin, made some fifty visits on the Row, examining each condemned inmate to determine his physical and mental status and to recommend any treatment that might be needed. In an interview he told me that at the end of this service he was left with the clear conclusion that, although the professional and custodial staff of the institution exert every reasonable and honest effort to make Death Row tolerable both to its inmates and to the staff, its grim mechanics turn it into a form of punishment as cruel as any man has yet devised.

Death Row is a shock, he said, for nearly all of the

inmates placed there. For those with a potential for growth and rehabilitation, the shock may actually cause the inmate to think seriously for the first time in his life, to learn to read and write, to understand the world about him better. In these cases the cruelty of Death Row and of capital punishment lies more in the fact that we are then executing not the original criminal but a redeemed man. In more cases, however, the shock of Death Row results in accelerating the process of mental deterioration.

Dr. Graves cited the case of Henry Ford McCracken, a man whose tiny head caused Graves to regard him as a probable microcephalic: "During his stay on Death Row, McCracken became no more than a vegetable. On one occasion I found him wallowing on the floor of his cell in his own excreta babbling incoherently. I arranged to have him transferred to the prison hospital where he was given electric shock therapy - this to bring him to a point of sanity at which he might be considered able to understand that he was being punished at the time of his execution."

Graves commented that others intelligent enough to understand their fate fought furiously, both mentally and emotionally, against it: "I remember Gilliam. When I saw him first, seated at the rear of his cell hunched over his small table with great beads of sweat literally pouring from his face onto the open Bible he was studying, I was accompanied by a prison official who handed him a court document....He took the document. The attendant attempted to console him. This was quite fruitless. He returned to his Bible to literally sweat out the remaining few days before the date scheduled for his execution. As I recall it, he did eventually receive a brief stay, only some weeks later to again go through a similar period of agony in expectation of the State's taking his life on an appointed day at an appointed hour."

Our society is based on a belief in the inherent dignity of man. Surely anything which undermines that dignity must be viewed as abhorrent to it. There is no need to relate more of these morbid vignettes.

APPENDIX B

A Model of the Process Producing Support for the Death Penalty[1]

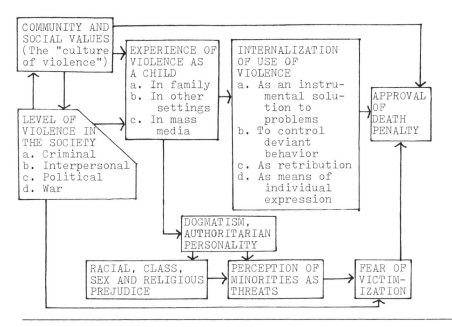

A Model of the Process Producing Support for the Death Penalty[2]

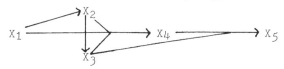

X_1=Perception of Crime Rate
X_2=Fear of Victimization
X_3=Perception of the Effectiveness
       of Punishment

X_4=Willingness to Employ
       Punishment as a Re-
       sponse to Criminality
X_5=Support for Capital
       Punishment

[1]Richard J. Gelles and Murray A. Straus, "Family Experience and Public Support of the Death Penalty," in Capital Punishment in the United States, Bedau and Pierce (eds.), p.241.

[2]Charles W. Thomas and Samuel C. Foster, "A Sociological Perspective on Public Support for Capital Punishment," in Bedau and Pierce, p.184.

FOOTNOTES

Chapter One

[1]George Ryley Scott, The History of Capital Punishment, (London, 1950), 4.

[2]The "Danegeld" in English law was the obligatory re-compensatory fine if one killed a Dane.

[3]"an eye for an eye, a tooth for a tooth,...a life for a life."

[4]Literally, "The King's peace," the ideal that was upset if someone committed a crime.

[5]Scott, 5.

[6]Ibid.

[7]Ibid., 7.

[8]Ibid., 8.

[9]Ibid.

[10]Ibid., 38.

[11]Hugo Adam Bedau, ed., The Death Penalty in America, (Garden City, 1964), 2. (general introduction)

[12]Scott, 39-40.

[13]Bedau, Death Penalty, 2,4.

[14]Scott, 64.

[15]Bedau, Death Penalty, 3-4.

[16]The "proof" involved reciting the "Neck Verse" (Psalm LI), thus showing clerical status; Ibid., 4.

[17]Ibid., 4.

[18]Scott, xiv.

[19]Philip English Mackey, ed., Voices Against Death: American Opposition to Capital Punishment, 1787-1975, (New York, 1976), xiii.

[20]Bedau, Death Penalty, 5; Mackey, xi.

[21]Warren Weaver, Jr., "Death Penalty a 300-Year Issue in America, New York Times, July 3, 1976, 7.

[22]William J. Bowers, Executions in America, (Lexington, 1974), 173.

[23]Bedau, Death Penalty, 7; Of course, even more actions were punishable by death if a Negro slave committed them. Up until the Civil War though, the South followed seemingly contradictory approaches to treating the slave population. On the one hand, legislation became increasingly more restrictive vis a vis slave movements, rebellions, and white aid to Negroes, but on the other hand, the courts increasingly attributed more human rights to the slave in cases where he was either the victim or perpetrator of violence. (see State v. Negro Will, 1 Devereux and Battle's Law Reps., (North Carolina) 121 (1834); State v. Caesar, A Slave, 9 Iredell's Law Reps., (North Carolina) 391 (1849); Stanley Katz, American Legal History, case materials in History 385, Princeton University, Fall Semester, 1978-1979.)

[24]Furman v. Georgia, 408 U.S. 238, 33 L. Ed 2d 346, 92 S. Ct. 2726 (1972) at 335 (J. Marshall).

[25]Mackey, xi; Rhode Island, however, inevitably went its own way, and was the last state to ratify the Constitution.

[26]Bedau, Death Penalty, 6.

[27]Furman, 408 U.S. 238 at 335; Bedau, Death Penalty, 6.

[28]Mackey, xv.

[29]Scott, xiv.

[30]Weaver, New York Times, July 3, 1976, 7.

[31]Furman, 408 U.S. 238 at 336; Bedau, Death Penalty, 8.

[32]Michael Meltsner, Cruel and Unusual: The Supreme Court and Capital Punishment, (New York, 1973), 49.

[33]Bedau, Death Penalty, 8.

[34]Mackey, xvi, xvii; Besides Pennsylvania and New York, the states were Virginia (1796), Kentucky (1798), Vermont (1797), Maryland (1810), New Hampshire (1812) and Ohio (1815).

[35] _Furman_, 408 U.S. 238 at 337.

[36] Bedau, _Death Penalty_, 8-9.

[37] Weaver, New York _Times_, July 3, 1976, 7.

[38] Mackey, 41.

[39] _Furman_, 408 U.S. 238 at 337; Maine fully abolished
the death penalty in 1876, re-instituted it in 1883, and
then re-abolished it for good in 1887. (source: United
States, Bureau of Prisons, National Prisoner Statistics
Bulletin, No. 46, August 1971, _Capital Punishment_: 1930-
1970, table 16, p. 50.)

[40] Mackey, xxvi.; And in 1963, as a formality, this
provision also was eliminated.

[41] U.S., Bureau of Prisons, _Capital Punishment_: 1930-
1970, table 16, p. 50.

[42] Mackey, xxviii.

[43] Meltsner, 50.

[44] _Furman_, 408 U.S. 238 at 339; U.S. Bureau of Prisons,
Capital Punishment: 1930-1970, table 16, p. 50.; Most
executions, however, are not under federal jurisdiction.
The total number of federal executions since 1930 is 33,
with none coming after 1963 (table 15, 49). Nevertheless,
it would be misleading to underplay the example the federal government sets for the states in maintaining the
death penalty at all.

[45] U.S., Bureau of Prisons, _Capital Punishment_: 1930-
1970, table 16, p. 50.; Tennessee retained capital punishment for rape, and Arizona and North Dakota kept it for
treason.

[46] Weaver, New York _Times_, July 3, 1976, 7.; Mackey,
xxxiii-xxxiv.

[47] Mackey, xxxii.

[48] _Ibid._, xxxvi-xxxvii.

[49] Bedau, _Death Penalty_, 334.

[50] Ibid.

[51] New York _Times_, December 26, 1924, in Mackey, xxxiii-xxxiv.

[52] Mackey, xxxviii.; But then, what did the public know? After serving 33 years of a "life" sentence, Nathan Leopold in 1958 begged his parole board "to show me the mercy I did not show; give me the chance to try to be useful and to justify my existence." He was released and went to work for a tiny stipend in Puerto Rico as a hospital orderly. (source: James Avery Joyce, _Capital Punishment: A World View_, (New York, 1961), 235.

[53] Mackey, xxxviii-xxxix.

[54] U.S. Bueau of Prisons, _Capital Punishment: 1930-1970_, table 1, p. 8.

[55] Herbert L. Cobin, "Abolition and Restoration of the Death Penalty in Delaware," in Bedau, _Death Penalty_, 372.

[56] Delaware did not go on to execute anyone. Their last executions were before 1950 (U.S. Bureau of Prisons, _Capital Punishment: 1930-1970_, table 3, p. 10).

[57] U.S. Bureau of Prisons, National Prisoner Statistics Bulletin, No. 45, August 1969, _Capital Punishment: 1930-1968_, table 15, p. 30.; Actually, only six. Hawaii and Alaska joined the Union as abolitionist states.

[58] Bowers, 25-26.

[59] Ibid., 28.

[60] Ibid.

[61] Ibid.

[62] Actually, there was only one recorded example of "peine forte et dure" in Colonial history. Giles Cory was "pressed" to death in a 1692 Salem witchcraft trial, Scott, 152.

[63] Arthur Koestler, _Reflections on Hanging_, (London, 1956), 17.

[64] Paul Meskil, "The Electric Chair," in Irwin Isenberg, ed., _The Death Penalty_, The Reference Shelf, vol 49, no. 2, (New York, 1977), 98.

[65]Bedau, _Death Penalty_, 18.

[66]Scott Christianson, "Killing with Kindness," _Playboy_, (April 1979), 65.

[67]Scott, 59.

[68]Koestler, 16.

[69]"Controversy over Capital Punishment: Pro and Con," _Congressional Digest_, 52 (January 1973), 4.

[70]Bedau, _Death Penalty_, 22.

[71]Bowers, 11.

[72]Bedau, _Death Penalty_, 25, 27-8.

[73]Meltsner, 51.

[74]Philip English Mackey, "The Inutility of Mandatory Capital Punishment: An Historical Note," in Hugo Adam Bedau and Chester M. Pierce, eds., _Capital Punishment in the United States_, (New York., 1975, 1976), 49.

[75]_Ibid._, 50.

[76]Mackey, xxx.

[77]_Gallup Opinion Index_, report no. 82, April 1972, p. 14.

[78]Statement of Hugo Adam Bedau on behalf of the American Civil Liberties Union before U.S. House of Representatives, Committee on the Judiciary, Subcommittee no. 3, 10 a.m., 16 March 1972 in American Civil Liberties Union, Documents Legal Briefs, and Memorandums, Princeton University, Mudd Library, IX. p. 1-2.

[79]_Ibid._, 1.; England actually abolished capital punishment in 1969 for all non-wartime offenses (source: "Death Penalty: A World Survey," _U.S. News & World Report_, 70 (May 31, 1971), 38.

[80]New York _Times_, December 10, 1976, B7.

Chapter Two

[1]National Research Council, Panel on Research on Deterrent and Incapacitative Effects, Deterrence and Incapacitation: Estimating the Effects of Criminal Sanctions on Crime Rates, (Washington, D.C., 1978), 3.

[2]Thorsten Sellin, The Death Penalty, (Philadelphia, 1959), 34.

[3]He had ten states to work with, one of which, Maine, abolished, restored, and reabolished the death penalty. (source: U.S. Bureau of Prisons, Capital Punishment: 1930-1970, table 16, p. 50).

[4]Thorsten Sellin, Capital Punishment, (New York, 1967), 124.

[5]Ibid., 146, 154.

[6]Study cited in Walter C. Reckless, "The Use of the Death Penalty: A Factual Statement," in James A. McCafferty, ed., Capital Punishment, (Chicago, 1972), 58-59.

[7]Leonard D. Savitz, "The Deterrent Effect of Capital Punishment in Philadelphia," in Bedau, Death Penalty, 321.

[8]Isaac Ehrlich, "The Deterrent Effect of Capital Punishment: A Question of Life and Death," American Economic Review, 65 (1975), 397, cited in Ernest van den Haag, Punishing Criminals, (New York, 1975), 217.

[9]See generally, William J. Bowers and Glenn L. Pierce, "The Illusion of Deterrence in Isaac Ehrlich's Research on Capital Punishment," in Bedau and Pierce, 372-395.; Also see Peter Passel's work, which using similar econometric techniques led him to conclude: "Students of capital punishment must look elsewhere for evidence confirming deterrence. We know of no reasonable way of interpreting the cross-section data that would lend support to the deterrence hypothesis." cited in National Research Council, 341-342.

[10]National Research Council, 12.

[11]Charles L. Black, Jr., Capital Punishment: The Inevitability of Caprice and Mistake, (New York, 1974), 26.

[12]Richard E. Gerstein, "A Prosecutor Looks at Capital Punishment," in McCafferty, 131.

[13]As the National Council on Crime and Delinquency's Journal noted: "Fear of arrest and imprisonment deters many from crime; fear of long imprisonment does not," in Eugene Doleschal, "The Deterrent Effect of Legal Punishment, A Review of the Literature," Information Review on Crime and Delinquency, I, 7, p. 4., ACLU Documents, Mudd Library, III.

[14]van den Haag, 216.

[15]The reasons are most aptly described by Anthony Amsterdam, "Capital Punishment: Do We Really Need to Kill People to Teach People That Killing is Wrong?" Vital Speeches of the Day, 43 (September 1, 1977), 681; see also Congressional Digest, 24.

[16]Bedau, Death Penalty, 267

[17]There are many more cases of these people than I care to document here. See generally Washington Research Project, The Case Against Capital Punishment, (Washington, 1971), 15; Mackey, 294; Bedau and Pierce, 439.

[18]New York Times, February 1, 1970, 44 in ACLU Documents, Mudd Library, XXXII.

[19]New York Times, November 15, 1976, 24, and December 14, 1976, 16.

[20]New York Times, November 15, 1976, 24.

[21]See for example the case of George Jackson, incarcerated on a capital charge, who claimed he had nothing to lose and shot his way out of prison, killing six. In Amsterdam, "Capital Punishment," 22.

[22]Edward J. Allen, "Capital Punishment: Your Protection and Mine," McCafferty, 118.

[23]Gerstein, Ibid., 138.

[24]Bowers, 160-161, and Bedau, Death Penalty, 36. It should be noted that the likelihood of significantly improving upon these rates of execution is minimal, given the present judicial concern with due process of the law.

[25]Sellin, *Capital Punishment*, 124.

[26]Great Britain, Royal Commission on Capital Punishment, *1949-1953 Report*, (London, 1953), 328-330.

[27]Cited in U.S., Congress, House Committee on the Judiciary, Subcommittee no. 3. 92 Congress, 2 session, *Capital Punishment*, (Washington, D.C., 1972), 24.

[28]*Furman*, 408 U.S. 238 at 301.

[29]Phoebe C. Ellsworth and Lee Ross, "Public Opinion and Judicial Decision Making: An Example From Research on Capital Punishment," in Bedau and Pierce, 168.

[30]Koestler, 105.

[31]Ellsworth and Ross, "Public Opinion," 168.

[32]Columbia Broadcasting System, Evening News Report, January 17, 1977, p. 1-2, Microfiche, Princeton University, Firestone Library.

[33]You might be asked to justify your viewpoint as moral, however. Ronald Dworkin in his article, "Lord Devlin and the Enforcement of Morals, 75 *Yale Law Journal* 986, (1966)(in Paul Brest, *Processes of Constitutional Decisionmaking: Cases and Materials*, (Boston, 1975), 935-937) has suggested a framework for such analysis. First, you have to produce some reasons for your view. This reason merely has to be some aspect of revenge which moves you to regard it as moral: saying the Bible calls for it, for example. In that this reason presupposed the underlying acceptance of some general principle or theory, however (e.g. the Bible shows us how to conduct our lives), the question of your sincerity and consistency come into play. Do you actually believe the injunctions of the Bible to be binding? And if this point is satisfied, do your other actions conform to this conduct? There can be exceptions in your behavior, but only if they, too, are backed by valid reasons. Otherwise you would merely be acting inconsistently.

If, for example, your mother is killed by your father, can you distinguish between foresaking revenge in that case and pursuing it if she had been killed by a mugger? Contending that your father has greater potential for rehabilitation, for example, may be arguable as a question of fact. Contending that you love your father more may have to be rejected as a personal emotional reaction. The moral position (revenge is good) is supposed to justify your emotional reaction (I _want_ revenge), and not vice versa.

All of which is not to say that the desire for revenge is an untenable moral position. You may _wish_ to kill your father in the above situation, or you may be able to reasonably _explain_ your reluctance to do so. The point is merely that to justify your belief in revenge as moral will require more than just feeling it is so.

[34]Koestler, 106.

[35]_Williams_ v. _New York_, 337 U.S. 241 (1949) at 248.

[36]_Furman_, 408 U.S. 238 at 343.

[37]New York _Post_, January 15, 1979, 5.

[38]One study asked people to rank the relative severities of a range of punishments. The result was that the greatest gap in perceived severity was between life imprisonment with the possibility of parole after twenty years and life imprisonment with no possibility of parole. The gap was small in perceived severity between life imprisoment without parole and a death sentence. See V. Lee Hamilton and Laurence Rotkin, "Interpreting the Eighth Amendment: Perceived Seriousness of Crime and Severity of Punishment," in Bedau and Pierce, 520.

[39]Jack P. Gibbs, "The Death Penalty, Retribution and Penal Policy," _Journal_ _of_ _Criminal_ _Law_ _&_ _Criminology_, 69 (Fall 1978) 295-296.

[40]_Furman_,U.S. 238 at 304 (J. Brennan).

[41]"Death Row Interviews," _U.S._ _News_ _&_ _World_ _Report_, 81 (July 12, 1976), 51.

[42]Black, 21; e.g. "Was the action of which the defendant was found guilty performed in such a manner as to evidence an 'abandoned and malignant' heart?" at p. 19.

[43]The following analysis is primarily based on Professor Charles L. Black, Jr.'s excellent book, _supra_ note 11.

[44]Black, 43.

[45]Bernard Laude Cohen, Law Without Order: Capital Punishment and the Liberals, (New Rochelle, 1970), 181.

[46]Gregg v. Georgia, 428 U.S. 153, 49 L. Ed 2d 859, 96 S. Ct. 2909, (1976) at 206.

[47]Jurek v. Texas, 428 U.S. 262, 49 L. Ed 2d 929, 96 S. Ct. 2950, (1976) at 272; also U.S. Congress, Senate Committee on the Judiciary, Subcommittee on Criminal Law and Procedures. 95 Congress, 1 session, To Establish Constitutional Procedures for the Imposition of Capital Punishment, (Washington, D.C., 1977), 315.

[48]Black, 63.

[49]New York Times, July 19, 1972, 15.

[50]"Question and Answer Session with Chief Justice Richard J. Hughes of the New Jersey Supreme Court," Frelinghuysen Room, Firestone Library, March 14, 1979.

[51]Black, 93.

[52]Washington Research Project, 49.

[53]Ibid.

[54]Black, 30.

[55]Cited in Ibid., 35.

[56]Ibid., 91.

[57]Michael DiSalle, The Power of Life or Death, (New York, 1965), 10; also U.S. Congress, Senate Committee on the Judiciary, Subcommittee on Criminal Law and Procedures, 93 Congress, 1 session, Imposition of Capital Punishment, (Washington, D.C., 1973), 84.

[58]Trevor Thomas, "This Life We Take," in U.S. Congress, House Report 1972, 371.

[59]Furman, 408 U.S. 238 at 251-252.

[60]Washington Research Project, 51.

[61]Marvin E. Wolfgang; Arlene Kelly; Hans C. Nolde; "Executions and Commutations in Pennsylvania," Bedau, Death Penalty, 464-488, gives precise statistics.

[62]U.S. Bureau of Prisons, Capital Punishment: 1930-1968, table 3, p. 10.

[63]Ibid., table 3, p. 10-11.

[64]The data and subsequent analysis are obtainable in: "Rape: Selective Electrocution Based on Race," in ACLU Documents, Mudd Library, XXXII; Marvin E. Wolfgang, "Racial Discrimination in the Death Sentence for Rape," Bowers, 104-120, taken from U.S. Congress, House Report 1972, 174-183; Marvin E. Wolfgang and Marc Riedel, "Rape, Racial Discrimination and the Death Penalty," in Bedau and Pierce, 99-121.

[65]Bowers, 120; Wolfgang and Riedel, 118.

[66]Bowers, 120.

[67]See, for example, Washington Research Project, 51-52; Bowers, 71-108; Marc Riedel, "Pre-Furman and Post-Furman: Comparisons and Characteristics of Offenders Under Death Sentences," Bedau and Pierce, 535-554; also supra note 61.

[68]It should be noted that in the 1977 case of Coker v. Georgia, the Supreme Court outlawed, under the Eighth Amendment's "Cruel and Unusual" punishment clause, the imposition of the death penalty in rape cases. Discrimination was not a factor for the majority.

[69]U.S. Bureau of Prisons, Capital Punishment: 1930-1968, table 3, p. 10-11.

[70]"Rape: Selective Electrocution Based on Race," charts A and B, in ACLU Documents, Mudd Library, XXXII.

[71]Wolfgang and Riedel, 111.

[72]Ibid.

[73]Wayne King, "Few on 3 Death Rows Are There for Killing Blacks," New York Times, March 6, 1978, A11.

[74]Ibid.

[75]Sexual discrimination appears to be an area for more research, too. Current data is insufficiently detailed for positive conclusions, but the statistics speak for themselves. Thirty-two out of 3859 executions since 1930 have been of women, but it is estimated that females commit about 15% of all homicides. (source: U.S. Bureau of

Prisons, Capital Punishment: 1930-1968, tables 3, 14, pp. 10, 48; also William O. Hochkammer, Jr., "The Capital Punishment Controversy," in McCafferty, 68). The problem is that there are no sure figures on what percentage of capital crimes women commit.

[76]Richard A. McGee, "Capital Punishment as Seen by a Correctional Administrator," in McCafferty, 163.

[77]Stanton, "Murderers on Parole," 15 Crime and Delinquency 149 (1969) cited in Washington Research Project, 20.

[78]Hon. James R. Browning (Judge, U.S. Court of Appeals for the Ninth Circuit), "The New Death Penalty Statutes: Perpetuating a Costly Myth," Gonzaga Law Review, 9 (Spring 1974), 697, ACLU Documents, Mudd Library, II.

[79]Bedau, Death Penalty, 398.

[80]DiSalle, 3.

[81]Stanton, in Washington Research Project, 20-21.

[82]See generally Sara R. Ehrmann, "The Human Side of Capital Punishment," in Bedau, Death Penalty, 492-519.

[83]Browning, 695.

[84]See generally Washington Research Project, 21-23.

[85]New York Times, December 6, 1976, 22.

[86]For accounts of such cases see: Bedau, "Murder, Errors of Justice, and Capital Punishment," in Bedau, Death Penalty, 434-452; Sara R. Ehrmann, "For Whom the Chair Waits," in McCafferty, 197-201;and James V. Bennet, "The Death Penalty," in McCafferty, 143. It is generally conceded that there are probably executions of innocent people which have not been uncovered simply because the impetus to find the truth is lost; see Browning, 657.

[87]Stein v. New York, 346 U.S. 156 at 196 (1953) in Washington Research Project, 55.

[88]Doleschal, 4.

[89]These costs are financial too. Despite some retentionists' claim that they don't wish to have their tax dollars spent to support murderers, "When all is

said and done, there can be no doubt that it costs more
to execute a man than to keep him in prison for life."
(Justice Marshall, Furman, 408 U.S. 238 at 358). For
example, it cost the state of California well over one
half million to execute Caryl Chessman in 1960 at a time
when annual costs to keep a prisoner incarcerated were
less than three thousand dollars. (Statement of Hugo Adam
Bedau, ACLU Documents, IX, 13). The costs are many:
lengthy trials; numerous appeals with transcripts provided
by the State; clemency hearings; issuance of stays; maintenance of maximum security Death Row cells in which
prisoners are kept many years; the fact that condemned men
are not allowed to work to offset these costs; the disproportionate time prison officials and judges spend on
death cases; multiple sanity determinations; and the actual
execution.

[90] van den Haag, 213.

[91] Frank G. Carrington, Neither Cruel nor Unusual, (New
Rochelle, 1978), 75.

[92] J. Edgar Hoover, "Statements in Favor of the Death
Penalty," in Bedau, Death Penalty, 132.

[93] Congressional Digest, 26.

[94] Colin Turnbull, "Death by Decree," Natural History,
87 (May 1978), 51.

[95] Most recently, condemned murderer John Louis Evans,
3rd., was granted a weeklong stay of death five hours before his execution time. On being informed of the short
reprieve, his first words were: "I will have to go through
this again." Then he wept.; Wayne King, "Alabamian Granted
a Supreme Court Stay," New York Times, April 6, 1979, A15.

[96] See generally: Washington Research Project, 29-40;
Burton H. Wolfe, Pile-up on Death Row, (New York, 1973),
41-56; Scott, part III; Roy Meador, Capital Revenge: 54
Votes Against Life, (Philadelphia, 1975), 183-199.

[97] Albert Camus, Resistance, Rebellion and Death, (New
York, 1961), 187.

Chapter Three

[1]George H. Gallup, The Gallup Poll: Public Opinion 1935-1971, 3 vols, (New York, 1972), vol 2, 1187.

[2]New York Times, November 23, 1972; Gallup Opinion Index, report no. 82, (April 1972), 14; also Gallup, Public Opinion 1935-1971, vol 3, 1922, 2016.

[3]Both Luis José Monge (1967) and Gary Gilmore (1977) waived their right to appeal and demanded to be executed. James French, the only man to be executed in 1966, acted similarly.

[4]U.S. Bureau of Prisons, Capital Punishment: 1930-1968, table 1, p. 7.

[5]U.S. Congressional Record, Proceedings and Debates of the 89th Congress, 2 session, "Abolition of the Federal Death Penalty," speech by the Senator from Michigan, Hon. Phillip A. Hart, July 25, 1966, in ACLU Document, Princeton University, Mudd Library, III.

[6]U.S. Bureau of Prisons, Capital Punishment: 1930-1970, table 16, p. 50.

[7]New York Times, April 10, 1960, 57.

[8]Ibid., July 3, 1968, 1, 24.

[9]Rudolph v. Alabama, 375 U.S. 308 (1963).

[10]Dr. Harry Elmer Barnes, cited in Joyce, 27.

[11]Joyce, 26; Wolfe, 102,3.

[12]Wolfe, 102-105; also see pp. 422-425 for an analysis of the complexities of the Little Lindbergh Law.

[13]Wolfe, 102; Joyce, 27; see the cases of Brown v. Mississippi, 297 U.S. 278 (1936), McNabb v. U.S. 318 U.S. 332 (1943), Mallory v. U.S., 354 U.S. 449 (1957).

[14]Wolfe, 107, Joyce, 28-29.

[15]See People v. Morse, 60 Cal. 2d 631, 338 P. 2d 33 (1964).

[16]See Chessman v. Teets, 354 U.S. 156, 1 L. Ed 2d 1253 (1957), at 1257-1258; also Wolfe, 111-112.

[17]Chessman v. Teets, 35 Cal 2d 455, 218 P. 2d 769 at 468-473; also cited in Wolfe, 113.

[18]Wolfe, 112-113.

[19]Chessman, 354 U.S. 156 at 1257 of 1 L. Ed 2d.

[20]Ibid., at 1261, 1263.

[21]Caryl Chessman, Trial by Ordeal, (Englewood Cliffs, 1955), back cover.

[22]Ibid., 46, 76.

[23]Wolfe, 114.

[24]Grant S. McClellan, ed., Capital Punishment, (New York, 1961), 116,118.

[25]New York Times, May 3, 1960, 1, 22-23.

[26]Joyce, 33, 208.

[27]Gerald Johnson, "Chessman's Challenge," New Republic, 142 (Mar. 7, 1960), 14.

[28]New York Times, February 20, 1960, 1, 12.

[29]Richard Meister, "Who Hates Chessman," Nation, 190 (February 20, 1960), 167-169.

[30]Wolfe, 121.

[31]New York Times, October 20, 1959, 27.

[32]Editorial, "Must Chessman Die?" New Republic, 142 (March 28, 1960), 3-4.

[33]New York Times, October 18, 1959, 66.

[34]Mcister, "Who Hates Chessman?" 168.

[35]See generally "The Press wants Chessman Dead," Californian, (May 1960).

[36]Wolfe, 118.

[37]New York Times, October 18, 1959, 66.

[38] See *Miranda* v. *Arizona*, 384 U.S. 436 (1965) and *Escobedo* v. *Illinois*, 378 U.S. 478 (1964).

[39] Los Angeles *Times*, May 25, 1954 and October 16, 1958, cited in Joyce, 46.

[40] Meister, "Who Wants Chessman Dead?" 168-169.

[41] Wolfe, notes on pp. 107-108.

[42] It would not be entirely unreasonable to liken the fear caused by the Red Light Bandit to that spread by New York's Son of Sam. Both inexplicably and randomly preyed on couples parked in cars. David Berkowitz, however, was publicly viewed as crazy, while Caryl Chessman was not.

[43] Joyce, 49-50.

[44] Richard Meister, "Politics and Chessman," *Nation*, 190 (March 26, 1960), 276.

[45] Chessman, *Trial*, 297.

[46] Clinton T. Duffy with Al Hirshberg, *88 Men and 2 Women*, (New York, 1962), 255.

[47] John Laurence, *A History of Capital Punishment*, (New York, 1960), xxv.

[48] Wolfe, 123.

[49] It continues to do so today. A TV Drama of Chessman's life, conviction and execution entitled "Kill Me if You Can," was aired as recently as September 1977.

[50] George H. Gallup, "Growing Trend Against Death Penalty Found in Canada, U.S.," *Public Opinion News Service*, (March 25, 1960), cited in McClellan, 95-96.

[51] James R. Christopher, *Capital Punishment and British Politics*, (Chicago, 1962), 100-105.

[52] Richard J. Gelles and Murray A. Strauss, "Family Experience and Public Support of the Death Penalty," in Bedau and Pierce, 233-235. Nevertheless, Appendix B gives an idea as to how support for the death penalty might be produced.

[53]Gallup, Public Opinion 1935-1971, vol 3, 1982,1993, 2007, 2027, 2074.

[54]Meltsner, 36.

[55]See Cooper v. Aaron, 358 U.S. 1 (1958), Aaron v. Cooper, 261 F. 2d 97 (1958) in Katz, American Legal History, case materials for History 385, Princeton University, Fall Semester 1978-1979.

[56]Carll Tucker, "Death on the Comeback Trail," Saturday Review, 5 (April 29, 1978), 56.; also Eric Goldman, "Modern America," History 377 Lectures, Princeton University, Fall Semester 1978-1979.

[57]Gallup, Public Opinion 1935-1971, vol 3, 1905.

[58]Meltsner, 40, 43.

[59]Of course, people tend to elect leaders who will represent their viewpoints, but there are nevertheless many "undecideds" or "no opinions" who are particularly susceptible to leadership influence.

[60]For a study of the problems of polls, see Polls: Their Use and Misuse in Politics, by Charles W. Roll, Jr., and Albert H. Cantril, (New York: Basic Books, 1972).

[61]Neil Vidmar and Phoebe Ellsworth, "Public Opinion and the Death Penalty," Stanford Law Review, 26 (June, 1974), 1245-1270, page 1248 in particular.

[62]Ibid., 1266.

[63]Gallup, Public Opinion 1935-1971, vol 3, 2086.

[64]Alan Blinder, "The Uneven History of American Fiscal Policy," Economics 101 Lecture, Princeton University, Spring Semester, 1978-1979, March 20, 1979, McCosh 10 Hall.

[65]Gallup, Public Opinion 1935-1971,; the polls on pp. 1595, 1894, 1934, 1966, 2009 indicate people's lack of concern about crime. The last two percentages are from 2128 and 2151.

[66]Charles W. Thomas and Samuel C. Foster, "A Sociological Perspective on Public Support for Capital Punishment," in Bedau and Pierce, 187.

[67]Gallup Opinion Index, report no. 132, (July 1976), 24; unfortunately, no national polls were taken on the issue between 1966 and 1969, so one can't specifically pinpoint where the turnaround occured.

[68]Browning, "The New Statutes," 669 quotes this foolishness.

[69]Ibid., fortunately he also refutes in on p. 670.

[70]Editorial, New York Times, January 5, 1973, 28.

[71]Increasing punitiveness and dissatisfaction with the courts are show in Gallup, Public Opinion, 1935-1971, pp. 1935, 2108, 2182. The question asked was: "In general, do you think the courts in this area deal too harshly, or not harshly enough with criminals?"

	April '65	Feb. '68	Jan. 69
Not Harsh:	48%	63%	75%
Too Harsh:	2%	2%	2%
Just Right:	34%	19%	13%

Chapter Four

[1]The National Association for the Advancement of
Colored People (NAACP) and the Legal Defense Fund (LDF)
had initially separated solely for tax reasons. They
were equally dedicated to the black man's plight in
America, but the LDF had the role of pursuing litigation,
while the NAACP focused on lobbying.

[2]Gerald H. Gottlieb, On Capital Punishment, pamphlet
in ACLU Documents, Mudd Library, XXXII.; also Meltsner, 17-
18.

[3]Meltsner, 36.

[4]Jack Greenberg and Jack Himmelstein, "Varieties of
Attack on the Death Penalty," in McCafferty, 234.

[5]Ibid., 235-236.

[6]Wolfe, 244-245.

[7]Carrington, 74.

[8]The details of this story were related to the author
by member of the New York Bar Association, Peter Gregory
Schwed, but can be confirmed in Wolfe, 232.

[9]U.S Bureau of Prisons, Capital Punishment: 1930-
1968, chart 2, p. 5.; Meltsner, 130.

[10]Meltsner, 129-130.

[11]Ibid., 130.

[12]Ibid., 130, 138.

[13]Letter from Jack Greenberg to Melvin Wulf, July 21,
1967, ACLU Documents, Mudd Library, XXXII.

[14]Letter from Anthony Amsterdam to William Friedlander,
January 23, 1969, Ibid.

[15]"Documents for proceeding in Federal Habeas Corpus
in a Capital Case in Which Execution is Imminent," Ibid.

[16]Meltsner, 109.

[17]Memorandum from Florence Robin to Melvin Wulf, May 8, 1968, ACLU Documents, Mudd Library,; The memo reported on the national LDF conference. The Fund, because of its special tax status, was forbidden from lobbying.

[18]See "Poll of ACLU Due Process Committee on Capital Punishment," December 9, 1963; "Memo of May 4, 1964,"; and June 20, 1965 News Release,; all in ACLU Documents, Mudd Library, XXXII.

[19]Letter from Eleanor Norton to Melvin Wulf, cc: Alan Reitman, July 5, 1967; reply from Alan Reitman to Eleanor Norton, July 11, 1967, ACLU Documents, *Ibid*.

[20]Robin to Wulf, May 8, 1968, *Ibid*.

[21]*Ibid*。

[22]*supra* chapter three, notes 13 and 38

[23]These arguments can be found in: Washington Research Project; Meltsner; Wolfe; U.S. Congress, House 1972 Report; *Witherspoon* v。 *Illinois*, 391 U.S. 510; *Maxwell* v. *Bishop*, 398 U.S. 262; *McGautha* v. *California*, 402 U.S. 183; *Furman* v. *Georgia*, 408 U.S. 238; and a number of legal briefs in the ACLU Documents, Mudd Library.

[24]See *Brown* v. *Board of Education*, 347 U.S. 483 (1954).

[25]Robin to Wulf, May 8, 1968, ACLU Documents, Mudd Library.

[26]The Fifth Amendment reads in part: "Nor shall any person be subject for the same offence to be twice put in jeopardy of *life* or *limb*;" (emphasis added). The Fourteenth Amendment, Section One, reads in part: "Nor shall any state deprive any person of *life*, liberty, or property, without due process of law;" (emphasis added). See Brest, 1347, 1349.

[27]*In Re Kemmler*, 136 U.S. 436 at 447 (1890)

[28]*Louisiana ex rel Francis* v. *Resweber*, 330 U.S. 853 (1947).

[29]*Trop* v. *Dulles*, 356 U.S. 86 (1958).

[30]*Ibid*。, at 101,100.

[31] Robinson v. California, 370 U.S. 660 (1962).

[32] Meltsner, 179-180.

[33] U.S. v. Jackson, 390 U.S. 570, 20 L. Ed 2d 138, 88 S. Ct. 1209. (1968).

[34] Ibid., at 138 of Lawyer's Edition 2d. Numerous state "Little Lindbergh Laws", including the California one under which Chessman had been executed, would be set aside as a result of this ruling in later challenges.

[35] Witherspoon v. Illinois, 391 U.S. 510, 20 L. Ed 2d 776, 88 S. Ct. 1770. (1968).

[36] Wolfe, 256.

[37] Witherspoon, at 780, L. Ed. 2d.

[38] New research has since come to light, however. See George L. Jurow, "New Data on the Effect of a 'Death Qualified' Jury on the Guilt Determination Process," in Bedau and Pierce, 461-501.

[39] Meltsner, 125.

[40] Boykin v. Alabama, 395 U.S. 238, 23 L. Ed 2d 274, 89 S. Ct. 1709. (1969).

[41] Meltsner, 184.

[42] See Maxwell v. Bishop, 257 F. Supp. 710 (1966); Maxwell v. Bishop, 398 F. 2d 138 (Eighth Circuit, 1968).

[43] Maxwell v. Bishop, 398 U.S. 262, 26 L. Ed 2d 221, 90 S. Ct. 1578 (1970).

[44] Wolfe, 291.

[45] Brief for petitioner in Maxwell v. Bishop, 26 L. Ed 2d at 862.

[46] McGautha v. California; Crampton v. Ohio; 402 U.S. 183, 28 L. Ed 2d 711, 91 S. Ct. 1454, numbered (203) and (204) respectively. The two cases are collectively referred to as McGautha. (1971).

[47] Meltsner, 228.

[48]Ralph v. Warden, 438 F. 2d 786 (1970), U.S. Court of Appeals, Fourth Circuit.

[49]Ibid., at 797.

[50]New York Times, December 30, 1970, 26; also Congressional Digest, 52 (Jan. 1973), 3.

[51]U.S Congress, House 1972 Report, 59; Meltsner, 236-237.

[52]McGautha, 402 U.S. 183, at 204.

[53]Ibid., at 213-217.

[54]Giaccio v. Pennsylvania, 382 U.S. 399 (1966)

[55]Ibid., at 402-403.

[56]McGautha, 402 U.S. 183, at 281.

[57]Ibid., at 282.

[58]Ibid., at 305, 309.

[59]Ibid., at 226.

[60]403 U.S. 952 (1971).

[61]State v. Funicello, 286 A. 2d 55 (1972), New Jersey Supreme Court; see also New York Times, January 18, 1972, 1, 15.

[62]Funicello v. State, 403 U.S. 948, 29 L. Ed 2d 859 (1971).

[63]State v. Funicello, at 66-67.

[64]People v. Anderson, 493 P. 2d 880, California Supreme Court (1972); see also New York Times, February 19, 1972, 1, 28.

[65]United States, National Criminal Justice Information and Statistics Service, National Prisoner Statistics Bulletin, Capital Punishment: 1971-1972, (December 1974).

[66]New York Times, February 19, 1972, 1, 28.

[67]"Attorneys for the NAACP Legal Defense and Educational Fund," in Mackey, Voices Against Death, 271, 274.

[68]Cited in Tom Wicker, "Death in California," New York Times, March 7, 1972, 39.

[69]Meltsner, 266.

[70]Ibid., 284-285.

[71]"Attorneys for the NAACP," Mackey, 271.

[72]This brief is best outlined in Meltsner, 250-251.

[73]New York Times, June 30, 1972, 1; Furman v. Georgia, 408 U.S. 238, 33 L. Ed 2d 346, 92 S. Ct. 2726 (1972).

[74]Committee Against Legalized Murder (CALM) Newsletter, VI (October 1972), 1, ACLU Document, Mudd Library, V.

[75]Furman, 408 U.S 238 at 256.

[76]Ibid., at 309.

[77]Ibid., at 397.

[78]See Austin Sarat and Neil Vidmar, "Public Opinion, the Death Penalty, and the Eighth Amendment: Testing the Marshall Hypothesis," Wisconsin Law Review, (1976, no. 1), 173.

[79]Furman, 408 U.S. 238 at 300.

[80]Ibid., at 369.

[81]The validity of Marshall's hypothesis was subsequently tested in several studies: see Sarat and Vidmar, supra note 78; Neil Vidmar and Phoebe Ellsworth, "Public Opinion and the Death Penalty," Stanford Law Review, 26 (June 1974), 1245-1270; Christopher T. Cory, "Pinning Down Vague Talk about the Death Penalty," Psychology Today, 12 (January 1979), 13; and Phoebe C. Ellsworth and Lee Ross, "Public Opinion and Judicial Decision Making: An Example From Research on Capital Punishment," in Bedau and Pierce, 152-189. The results were supportive of Marshall's theory: 1. people were substantially uninformed about the death penalty (Sarat and Vidmar, 185; Vidmar and Ellsworth, 1256; Ellsworth and Ross, 164); 2. Support for the death penalty diminished when it came down to a concrete situation (Vidmar

and Ellsworth, 1248-1251, Cory, 13); 3. Support for the
death penalty diminished when people were informed as to
the utilitarian aspects of capital punishment (Sarat and
Vidmar, 190); 4. A large degree of the support for capital
punishment was based on retributive urges. Among these
people, presentation of information as to the workings
and administration of capital punishment had little effect
(Sarat and Vidmar, 192-194; Vidmar and Ellsworth, 1256-
1257; Ellsworth and Ross, 168); 5. Discounting retributive
urges, which may or may not be legitimately legislated, at
least ten percent of the population was well out of step
with current notions of penology in expressing support
for a mandatory death penalty for all muggers and bank robbers (Vidmar and Ellsworth, 1250-1255); 6. Capital punishment is desirable even if the justice it dispenses is
not always fair. For example, although 58% of the public
felt that the death penalty should not be universally administered to pre- meditated murders, faced with the choice
between a completely mandatory death penalty and no death
penalty at all, the percentage rose to 63% (Ellsworth and
Ross, 167-168). For an interesting approach to interpreting
this last point, see John Rawls, A Theory of Justice, (Cam-
bridge: Harvard University Press, 1971).

[82]Sarat and Vidmar, 174.

[83]Furman, 408 U.S. 238 at 390 n. 12.

[84]Ibid., at 406, 410, 413.

[85]Ibid., at 456.

[86]Ibid., at 400.

[87]Ibid., at 269.

[88]New York Times, June 30, 1972, 15; for other optimistic
reactions, see Hugo Adam Bedau, The Courts, the Constitution,
and Capital Punishment, (Lexington, 1977), 90; Mackey, lii.

[89]Furman, 408 U.S. 238 at 401.

[90]See Furman at 401 (Burger) and 413 (Blackmun).

Chapter Five

[1]New York Committee to Abolish Capital Punishment, "Memorandum to All Members and Supporters," July 14, 1972, ACLU Documents, Mudd Library, XXXII.

[2]The number of states with mandatory laws can vary from about 13 to 17 depending on how one interprets their various provisions.

[3]See Jane C. England, "Capital Punishment in the Light of Constitutional Evolution: An Analysis of Distinctions Between *Furman* and *Gregg*," *Notre Dame Lawyer*, 51 (April 1976), 600-601 notes 29, 32, 33; also see New York *Times*, November 8, 1972, 40.

[4]New York *Times*: November 8, 1972, 40; December 9, 1972, 32; May 10, 1973, 18; December 30, 1973, 19; March 14, 1974, 1; Michael Meltsner, "Cruel and Unusual Punishment. October 11, 1974, 39; March 14, 1975, 39; March 31, 1976, 38; July 3, 1976, 7.

[5]*Gregg* v. *Georgia*, 428 U.S. 153, 49 L. Ed 2d 859, 96 S. Ct. 2909 (1976).

[6]*Ibid.*, at 169. Brennan and Marshall dissented. Douglas, who had retired after a stroke, had been replaced by the Gerald Ford appointee, John Paul Stevens, who along with Stewart, White and the Nixon appointees, constituted the majority in the decision.

[7]*Ibid.*, at 173.

[8]*Ibid.*, at 175.

[9]*supra* footnote 81, chapter four.

[10]*Gregg*, 428 U.S. 153, at 183.

[11]See Bedau, *The Courts*, 147, on this point.

[12]*Gregg*, 428 U.S. 153, at 195.

[13]*Ibid.*, at 199.

[14]*Furman*, 408 U.S. 238 at 257.

[15]*Gregg*, 428 U.S. 153, at 226.

[16] New York _Times_, March 31, 1976, 38.

[17] See _Proffitt_ v. _Florida_, 428 U.S. 242, 49 L. Ed 2d 913, 96 S. Ct. 2960 (1976); _Jurek_ v. _Texas_, 428 U.S. 262, 49 L. Ed 2d 929, 96 S. Ct. 2950 (1976).

[18] See Bedau, _The Courts_, 113, for a fuller analysis.

[19] See _Woodson_ v. _North Carolina_, 428 U.S. 280, 49 L. Ed 2d 944, 96 S. Ct. 2978 (1976); _Roberts_ v. _Louisiana_, 428 U.S. 325, 49 L. Ed 2d 974, 96 S. Ct. 3001 (1976).

[20] New York _Times_, July 3, 1976, 7.

[21] _Woodson_, 428 U.S. 280, at 304.

[22] _Ibid._, at 305.

[23] "The Death Penalty -- Issue That Won't Go Away," _U.S. News & World Report_, 82 (January 31, 1977), 47.

[24] _Ibid._

[25] New York _Times_, November 11, 1976, 1.

[26] See letter from Melvin Wulf to Florence Wills, November 27, 1973, ACLU Documents, Mudd Library, IV.

[27] New York _Times_, November 17, 1976, 31.

[28] _Newsweek_, 89 (January 24, 1977), 35.

[29] New York _Times_, November 11, 1976, 14.

[30] Tom Wicker, "The Fifth Cartridge," _Ibid._, November 19, 1976, A27.

[31] _Time_, 109, (January 31, 1977), 49.

[32] New York _Times_, November 11, 1976, 14.

[33] Robert Friedman, "Hell's Agent," _Esquire_, 88 (October 1977), 134; _Newsweek_, 89 (January 31, 1977), 77-78.

[34] Friedman, 134.

[35] Columbia Broadcasting System, Evening News Report, January 17, 1977, 1-2, Microfiche, Princeton University, Firestone Library; New York _Times_, January 18, 1977, 1, 21.

[36] CBS Evening News, January 17, 1977, 3.

[37] New York _Times_, May 9, 1977, 1, 59.

[38] _Ibid._, 59.; Delaware, Maryland and New Jersy had laws awaiting their governor's signatures. Since the _Woodson_ ruling had overturned mandatory statutes these figures were down from the 34 states and 611 prisoners at the time of _Gregg_.

[39] _Ibid._

[40] _Coker_ v. _Georgia_, 433 U.S. 584, 53 L. Ed 2d 982, 97 S. Ct. 2861 (1977), Burger and Rehnquist dissenting.

[41] _Ibid._, at 592.

[42] _Ibid._, at 593-596; two other states, Florida and Mississippi, had the death penalty for child rapists.

[43] _Ibid._, at 598.

[44] Bedau, _The Courts_, 115.

[45] _Ibid._

[46] _Gardner_ v. _Florida_, 430 U.S. 349, 51 L. Ed 2d 393, 97 S. Ct. 1197 (1977).

[47] _Lockett_ v. _Ohio_, 46 Law Week 4981, no. 76-6997 (1978).

[48] _Ibid._, at 4983.

[49] _Ibid._, at 4986.

[50] _Ibid._

[51] _Ibid._, at 4987.

[52] _Ibid._, at 4986.

[53] _Ibid._, at 4989.

[54] New York _Times_, July 16, 1978, IV, 9.

[55] _Lockett_, 46 L.W. 4981 at 4986.

[56] _Spenkelink_ v. _Wainwright_, No. 78-6048 (1979).

[57]Peter Ross Range, "Will He Be The First?" New York _Times_, March 11, 1979, VI, 78.

[58]_Ibid_.

[59]Jon Nordheimer, "Condemned Man to get Florida Clemency Hearing," New York _Times_, March 27, 1979, A22.

[60]New York _Times_, May 26, 1979, A1.

[61]_Ibid_., A6.

[62]An interesting statistic accompanying Spenkelink's execution was the murder rate in Florida for the first six months of 1979. It climbed 14%, despite the fact that this widely-publicized execution was Florida's first in fifteen years (See New York _Times_, August 17, 1979, A10). Unfortunately, there is very little useful interpretation to be had from this sort of figure. The percentage might have been higher without the execution, or perhaps the execution helped cause it to be as high as it was. Retentionists certainly would argue that a regular pattern of executions is needed before there is a noticeable effect on the murder rate. Suffice it to say, then, that the question of deterrence remained just as difficult to prove or disprove after Spenkelink's execution as before.

[63]New York _Times_, October 23, 1979, A1.

[64]_Ibid_.

[65]_Ibid_., March 9, 1981, A1.

[66]_Ibid_., March 7, 1981, 13.

[67]_Ibid_., August 10, 1982, A12 and August 11, 1982, A1.

[68]_Ibid_.

[69]Two such decisions, handed down by the Supreme Court in its Spring 1981 term, were _Estelle_ v. _Smith_ and _Bullington_ v. _Missouri_. In the former, a death row inmate was granted a new trial because a psychiatric evaluation, given in confidence, was later used against him by the prosecution. In the latter, a five-to-four decision, the Court extended the constitutional protection against double jeopardy to the criminal sentencing stage of a bifurcated trial. The

defendant had been found guilty and sentenced to life in prison, but had been granted a new trial based on certain technicalities. The decision meant that the prosecutor was not now free to push for the death penalty, even though there was to be a completely new trial (See New York Times, May 24, 1981, IV, 7 and May 5, 1981, B15 respectively).

[70] New York Times, June 14, 1981, 28.

[71] Ibid., July 20, 1982, A17.

[72] Ibid., December 7, 1982, A19.

[73] Ibid., A1 and A19.

[74] Ibid. Four states, in addition to Texas, presently allow for execution by lethal injection: Oklahoma; Idaho; New Mexico; and Washington. The procedure, however, has raised severe questions of medical ethics as doctors have become more intimately involved with the execution procedure, from supplying and/or recommending the deadly barbituate, sodium thiopental, to checking the capability of the inmate's veins for receiving a large enough catheter needle (Ibid.).

[75] New York Times, December 8, 1982, A28.

[76] Ibid., December 6, 1982, A16.

[77] Ibid., December 8, 1982, A28.

[78] Washington Post, December 8, 1982, A1.

[79] New York Times, January 25, 1983, A21.

[80] Ibid. The Court also asked for argument on a specific aspect of Barefoot's sentencing, namely the appropriateness of permitting the introduction of psychiatric predictions on the defendant's future potential as a danger to society if sentenced to prison and eventually released (Ibid.).

[81] New York Times, January 25, 1983, A21.

[82] Washington Post, January 25, 1983, A1.

[83] Robert G. McCloskey, The American Supreme Court, (Chicago, 1960), 223.

[84] U.S. Congress, House 1972 Report, 64.

[85] New York Times, July 15, 1976, 3.

[86] Trevor Beeson, "The British and the IRA," in Isenberg, ed., The Death Penalty, 80.

[87] Most recently, both France and Belgium have voted to abolish the death penalty. (See New York Times, October 1, 1981, 4 for France and Ibid., August 18, 1981, 5 for Belgium.)

[88] Both have vetoed death penalty legislation and expressed (and kept) the intention not to let any executions take place during their administrations.

[89] The Maine Law of 1837, discussed in chapter one, page 14, is a good example.

[90] "President Asks Law to Restore Death Penalty," New York Times, March 11, 1973, 1, 55.

[91] Carey, Brown and Cuomo, of course, are exceptions: see the New York Times, April 12, 1978 for the text of Carey's veto of New York's death penalty legislation; see Brown's similar statement at Ibid., January 7, 1977, 8.

[92] Gottlieb, preface.

[93] Perhaps, however, they can be channeled into the law without the necessity of executions. For example, juries might be permitted to return a sentence of death purely as a censuring or symbolic action, where the convict still would only be imprisoned, though probably for life without parole. It is possible that this or similar techniques might help to provide a suitable outlet for retributive urges.

BIBLIOGRAPHY

I. Primary Sources

  A) Official

    Great Britain. Royal Commission on Capital Punishment.
        1949-1953 Report. Her Majesty's Stationery Office.
        London, 1953.

    National Research Council. Panel on Research on
        Deterrent and Incapacitative Effects. Deterrence
        and Incapacitation: Estimating the Effects of
        Criminal Sanctions on Crime Rates. Washington, D.C.:
        National Academy of Sciences, 1978.

    New Jersey. Council to Abolish Capital Punishment.
        Twenty Questions on Capital Punishment. 1958.

    New Jersey. Legislature. Commission Appointed to
        Study Capital Punishment. Public Hearing Pursuant
        to Senate Joint Resolution no. 3. July 10, 1964.

    United States. Congress. House Committee on the
        Judiciary, Subcommittee no. 3. 92 Congress, 2 session.
        Capital Punishment. Washington, D.C.: U.S. Govern-
        ment Printing Office, 1972.

    United States. Congress. Senate Committee on the
        Judiciary, Subcommittee on Criminal Law and Pro-
        cedures. 93 Congress, 1 session. Imposition of
        Capital Punishment. Washington, D.C.: U.S. Govern-
        ment Printing Office, 1973.

    United States. Congress. Senate Committee on the
        Judiciary, Subcommittee on Criminal Law and Pro-
        cedures. 95 Congress, 1 session. To Establish
        Constitutional Procedures for the Imposition of
        Capital Punishment. Washington, D.C.: U.S. Govern-
        ment Printing Office, 1977.

    United States. Bureau of Prisons. National Prisoner
        Statistics Bulletin. No. 45, August 1969. Capital
        Punishment: 1930-1968.

United States. Bureau of Prisons. National Prisoner
Statistics Bulletin. No. 46, August 1971. Capital
Punishment: 1930-1970.

United States. National Criminal Justice Information
and Statistics Service. National Prisoner Statistics
Bulletin. December 1974. Capital Punishment: 1971-
1972.

United States. National Criminal Justice Information
and Statistics Service. National Prisoner Statistics
Bulletin. November 1977. Capital Punishment: 1976.

B) Court Cases

Ralph v. Warden. 438 F. 2d 786 (1970). U.S. Court
of Appeals, Fourth Circuit.

State v. Funicello. 286 A. 2d 55 (1972). New Jersey
Supreme Court.

People v. Anderson. 493 P. 2d. 880 (1972). California
Supreme Court.

Weems v. U.S. 217 U.S. 349 (1910).

Williams v. New York. 337 U.S. 241 (1949).

Trop v. Dulles. 356 U.S. 86 (1958).

Robinson v. California. 370 U.S. 660 (1962).

Rudolph v. Alabama. 375 U.S. 308 (1963).

Giaccio v. Pennsylvania 382 U.S. 399 (1966).

U.S. v. Jackson. 390 U.S. 570, 20 L. Ed 2d 138, 88 S.
Ct. 1209. (1968).

Witherspoon v. Illinois. 391 U.S. 510, 20 L. Ed 2d 776,
88 S. Ct. 1770. (1968).

Boykin v. Alabama. 395 U.S. 238, 23 L. Ed 2d 274, 89
S. Ct. 1709. (1969).

Maxwell v. Bishop. 398 U.S. 262, 26 L. Ed 2d 221, 90
S. Ct. 1578. (1970).

McGautha v. California. (203) 402 U.S. 183, 28 L. Ed 2d 711, 91 S. Ct. 1454. (1971).

Crampton v. Ohio. (204) 402 U.S. 183, 28 L. Ed 2d 711, 91 S. Ct. 1454. (1971).

Furman v. Georgia. 408 U.S. 238, 33 L. Ed 2d 346, 92 S. Ct. 2726. (1972).

Gregg v. Georgia. 428 U.S. 153, 49 L. Ed 2d 859, 96 S. Ct. 2909. (1976).

Jurek v. Texas. 428 U.S. 262, 49 L. Ed 2d 929, 96 S. Ct. 2950. (1976)

Proffitt v. Florida. 428 U.S 242, 49 L. Ed 2d 913, 96 S. Ct. 2960. (1976).

Woodson v. North Carolina. 428 U.S. 280, 49 L. Ed 2d 944, 96 S. Ct. 2978. (1976).

Roberts v. Louisiana. 428 U.S. 325, 49 L. Ed 2d 974, 96 S. Ct. 3001. (1976).

Coker v. Georgia. 433 U.S. 584, 53 L. Ed 2d 982, 97 S. Ct. 2861. (1977).

Gardner v. Florida. 430 U.S. 349, 51 L. Ed 2d 393, 97 S. Ct. 1197. (1977).

Lockett v. Ohio. 46 L.W. 4981, no. 76-6997. (1978).

C) Unpublished Documents

American Civil Liberties Union. Documents, Legal Briefs, and Memorandums. Princeton University, Mudd Library, Volumes II, III, IV, V, VI, IX, XXXII.

Doar, Fred. Capital Punishment: Cruel and Unusual. Senior Thesis, April 1977. Princeton University, Mudd Library.

D)   Newspapers and News Reports

Columbia Broadcasting System. Morning, Afternoon, and Evening News Reports. January - August 1977. Microfiche, Princeton University, Firestone Library.

New York <u>Post</u>. 1979.

New York <u>Times</u>. 1959-1960, 1970-1983, Microfilm,
   Princeton University, Firestone Library.

Washington <u>Post</u>. June 1977-December 1978, December
   1982-January 1983, Microfilm, Princeton University,
   Firestone Library.

E)   Periodicals

<u>Congressional Digest</u>. "Controversy over Capital
   Punishment: Pro and Con." Vol. 52, no. 1, Jan. 1973.

<u>Gallup Opinion Index</u>. 1965, 1970, 1972, 1976.

<u>Newsweek</u>. 1977.

<u>Time</u>. 1960, 1977.

<u>U.S. News & World Report</u>. 1971, 1976, 1977.

F)   Interviews

"Question and Answer Session with Chief Justice
   Richard J. Hughes of the New Jersey Supreme Court."
   Frelinghuysen Room, Firestone Library. March 14,
   1979, 8:00 p.m.

II.   <u>Secondary Sources</u>

   A)   Articles

   Amsterdam, Anthony G. "Capital Punishment: Do We
      Really Need to Kill People to Teach People that
      Killing is Wrong?" <u>Vital Speeches of the Day</u>.
      43 (Sept. 1, 1977), 677-682.

   Bedau, Hugo Adam. "New Life for the Death Penalty."
      <u>The Nation</u>. 223 (Aug. 28, 1976), 144-8.

   Christianson, Scott. "Killing with Kindness."
      Playboy. 82 (Jan. 31, 1977), 47.

Cory, Christopher T. "Pinning Down Vague Talk About the Death Penalty." Psychology Today. 12 (Jan. 1979), 13.

Editorial. "Must Chessman Die?" New Republic. 142 (Mar. 28, 1960), 3-4.

England, Jane C. "Constitutional Evolution: An Analysis of Distinctions Between Furman and Gregg." Notre Dame Lawyer. 52 (April 1977), 596.

Friedman, Robert. "Hell's Agent." Esquire. 88 (Oct. 1977), 75-78.

Gibbs, Jack P. "The Death Penalty, Retribution and Penal Policy." Journal of Criminal Law & Criminology. Northwestern University School of Law. 69 (Fall 1978), 291.

Johnson, Gerald. "Chessman's Challenge." New Republic. 142 (Mar. 7, 1960), 14.

Meister, Richard. "Politics and Chessman." Nation. 190 (Mar. 26, 1960), 275-7.

_____. "Who Hates Chessman?" Nation. 190 (Feb. 20, 1960), 167-9.

Pinsky, Mark. "Legal Aid in the 'Death Belt.'" Nation. 224 (Mar. 26, 1977), 367-8.

Sarat, Austin, and Vidmar, Neil. "Public Opinion, the Death Penalty, and the Eighth Amendment: Testing the Marshall Hypothesis." Wisconsin Law Review. Vol. 1976, no. 1, 171-206.

Tao, L.S. "Beyond Furman v. Georgia: the Need for a Morally Based Decision on Capital Punishment." Notre Dame Lawyer. 51 (April 1976), 722.

Thomas, Charles W. "Eighth Amendment Challenges to the Death Penalty: the Relevance of Informed Public Opinion." Vanderbilt Law Review. 30 (Oct. 1977), 1005.

Tucker, Carll. "Death on the Comeback Trail." Saturday Review. 5 (April 29, 1978), 56.

Turnbull, Colin. "Death by Decree." <u>Natural History</u>.
87 (May 1978), 51.

Vidmar, Neil, and Ellsworth, Phoebe. "Public Opinion
and the Death Penalty." <u>Stanford Law Review</u>. 26
(June 1974), 1245-1270.

Younger, Evelle J. "Capital Punishment: the People's
Mandate." <u>Vital Speeches of the Day</u>. 43 (Sept. 1,
1977), 682-6.

B)   Books

Bedau, Hugo Adam,(ed) <u>The Death Penalty in America</u>.
Garden City: Anchor Books, 1964.

Bedau, Hugo Adam. <u>The Courts, the Constitution, and
Capital Punishment</u>. Lexington: Lexington Books, 1977.

Bedau, Hugo Adam, and Pierce, Chester M.,(eds.).
<u>Capital Punishment in the United States</u>. New York:
AMS Press, 1975,6.

Black, Charles L. Jr. <u>Capital Punishment: the Inevitability of Caprice and Mistake</u>. New York: W.W. Norton
& Company, 1974.

Bowers, William J. <u>Executions in America</u>. Lexington:
Lexington Books, 1974.

Brest, Paul. <u>Processes of Constitutional Decision-
making: Cases and Materials</u>. Boston: Little,
Brown and Co., 1975.

Camus, Albert. <u>Resistance, Rebellion and Death</u>.
New York: Alfred A. Knopf, 1961.

Carrington, Frank G. <u>Neither Cruel nor Unusual</u>.
New Rochelle: Arlington House, 1978.

Chessman, Caryl. <u>Trial by Ordeal</u>. Englewood Cliffs:
Prentice Hall, 1955.

Christopher, James R. <u>Capital Punishment and British
Politics</u>. Chicago: University of Chicago Press, 1962.

Cohen, Bernard Laude. Law Without Order: Capital Punishment and the Liberals. New Rochelle: Arlington House, 1970.

DiSalle, Michael V. The Power of Life or Death. New York: Random House, 1965.

Duffy, Clinton T., with Hirshberg, Al. 88 Men and 2 Women. New York: Doubleday, 1962.

Gallup, George, H. The Gallup Poll: Public Opinion 1935-1971. 3 vols. New York: Random House, 1972.

_____. The Gallup Poll: Public Opinion 1972-1977. 2 vols. Scholarly Resources, Inc., 1978.

Isenberg, Irwin, (ed.). The Death Penalty. The Reference Shelf, vol 49, no. 2. New York: H.W. Wilson Co., 1977.

Johnson, Julia E., (ed.). Capital Punishment. The Reference Shelf, vol. 13, no. 1. New York: H.W. Wilson Co., 1939.

Joyce, James Avery. Capital Punishment: A World View. New York: Thoman Nelson & Sons, 1961.

Koestler, Arthur. Reflections on Hanging. London: Victor Gollancz Ltd., 1956.

Laurence, John. A History of Capital Punishment. New York: Citadel Press, 1960.

McCafferty, James A., (ed.). Capital Punishment. Chicago: Aldine/Atherton Inc., 1972.

McClellan, Grant S., (ed.). Capital Punishment. The Reference Shelf, vol 32, no 6. New York: H.W. Wilson Co., 1961.

McCloskey, Robert G. The American Supreme Court. Chicago: University of Chicago Press, 1960.

Meador, Roy. Capital Revenge: 54 Votes Against Life. Philadelphia: Dorrance & Co., 1975.

Mackey, Philip English., (ed.). Voices Against Death: American Opposition to Capital Punishment, 1787-1975. New York: Burt Franklin & Co., Inc., 1976.

Meltsner, Michael. <u>Cruel</u> <u>and</u> <u>Unusual</u>: <u>The</u> <u>Supreme</u>
   <u>Court</u> <u>and</u> <u>Capital</u> <u>Punishment</u>. New York: Random
   House, 1973.

Moberly, Sir Walter. <u>The</u> <u>Ethics</u> <u>of</u> <u>Punishment</u>. London:
   Faber and Faber, 1968.

Neate, Charles Esq. <u>Considerations</u> <u>on</u> <u>the</u> <u>Punishment</u>
   <u>of</u> <u>Death</u>. London: James Ridgway, Piccadilly, 1857.

Scott, George Ryley. <u>The</u> <u>History</u> <u>of</u> <u>Capital</u> <u>Punishment</u>.
   London: Torchstream Books, 1950.

Sellin, Thorsten. <u>Capital</u> <u>Punishment</u>. New York: Harper
   & Row, 1967.

_____. <u>The</u> <u>Death</u> <u>Penalty</u>. Philadelphia:
   American Law Institute, 1959.

van den Haag, Ernest. <u>Punishing</u> <u>Criminals</u>. New York:
   Basic Books, 1975.

Washington Research Project. <u>The</u> <u>Case</u> <u>Against</u> <u>Capital</u>
   <u>Punishment</u>. Washington: Washington Research Project,
   1971.

Wolfe, Burton H. <u>Pile-up</u> <u>on</u> <u>Death</u> <u>Row</u>. New York:
   Doubleday, 1973.

INDEX

For additional information, see Notes and Appendices.